Victory!

The Life of José M. Mejia

*God's Miracles
During the Civil War
in
El Salvador*

By

José Medardo Mejia
With Joan Cardoza

PRESS

Contents

Preface 4

Introduction 6

El Salvador 9

Invasion...16

Survival 29

Escape 37

The Ranch...45

A New Beginning...49

Life on the Ranch 52

A Home of Our Own 58

The Long Journey..66

In the Land of My Dreams 74

Answered Prayers..82

My Father is Saved 93

Looking Back..96

Acknowledgements 103

Appendix 108

Post Script..124

About the Author...130

Preface

In honor to God and in thankfulness of His Grace, I would like to share with you some of the many things that have happened in my life and how God has protected me and provided for all my needs and those of my family.

My prayer is that when you read this Autobiography-Testimony of my life, God will touch your heart in a special way and let you know that He is as real as the air we breathe every day.

What I am about to share with you is not a story that I heard from ancient days. This is a real Autobiography-Testimony of my life as I have lived it thus far. It is real, as the miracles are real, as God is real.

As I was gathering information during the writing of this book, I had the opportunity to ask my dad about his experiences. I told him that I was writing the story of my life and our family's life. He said, "Why do you want to bring such things back into our memories? That will only make our wounds bleed again."

I explained to him that through this book, I want to glorify God and honor Him by sharing with many people what God was able to do for us no matter where we had been or what circumstances had surrounded us.

Dad responded, "As I look back over my life, it is clear we could not have survived without the existence of someone or something above every human being on the planet. It is a miracle and much more than a blessing to have you and your brothers and sisters alive today. I don't know how much I can share with you, son, because this is so painful that I wish those memories were wiped from my mind forever, but because you have asked me to share with you, I will try."

So as you read about the journey of my life in these pages, I will also share with you the words given to me by my dad.

Before I continue, I am compelled to bring before the Lord the works He will provide in the hearts of all who read my story.

Father, in the name of Jesus Christ and for the power of the Holy Spirit, I lift my prayer to You with a deep request from the bottom of my heart. I come before Your throne to ask You, Father, that You give favor and a special touch to each person that is reading this book. Show them how real You are and how much You love them. Your word says in Romans 10:13 "for every one who calls on the name of the Lord will be saved." {NIV} One day I called on to You Lord and You saved me.

Thank You for the one person that You are touching right now, thank You for the fifty souls that are being saved, thank You for the hundreds that are praising You, and thank You for the millions of people that will come to You, Lord.

Blessed be Your name. Amen

Introduction

You are about to embark on an incredible journey. It may, at the outset, appear to be fictional. I assure you, this is not fiction by any stretch of the imagination. It is not meant to be sensationalistic prose designed to guilt one into a certain frame of thinking. On the contrary, it is a true story whose telling time has come. The author would never voluntarily endure revisiting his horrible past if it were not for the demonstrative purposes of enriching and encouraging the reader's faith in things unseen. You have heard the old adage, "Truth is stranger than fiction." The truth you are about to read could never have come from the mind of man; not even its outcome.

The second largest civil war in Latin America's history took the lives of an estimated 75,000 people. Among the atrocities was the El Mozote massacre in December of 1981. Many other indiscriminate civilian killings took place in this time period including bombings of the countryside and cold-blooded murder of innocents under a radical and politically-charged, fraudulent regime. Seeding these events in the late 1960s and early 1970s was extreme dissent and violence between the repressive government and it's people. In this small, war-torn country of El Salvador, a small boy grappled with the horror of mankind's relentless evil toward its fellow man. The sites and sounds of a happy home were stolen from his childhood and replaced with death and destruction. As he fought for survival under circumstances that most of us cannot possibly comprehend, José clung to an unknown force that drove him forward through life. He escaped military boundaries and checkpoints on his epic 3,000-mile walk to the United States with little food and water; his exceptional faith is often his only sustenance.

Something of miraculous proportions has given life to this man who should have died as a boy, yet lives. What's more, José does not just survive, he conquers his fear and he is victorious over all odds; divinely lead and watched over. By all measure, José should be a psychological poster child with the shattered home life and terrifying images that were seared into his brain as a toddler. Instead, this boy, now a man, has impacted so many lives in such a positive way, his story has to be read over and over for the magnitude of his victory to be fully appreciated.

A great deal of effort has been put forth to bring you José's story. Several people—some were angels of God, I suspect—were made to cross paths with José that his story might come to life in the pages of this book. Because of the very personal nature of an autobiography, painstaking editing has been applied to retain the unique personal construct of the way José speaks. The sentences and wording are his own and were changed only when necessary to clarify the imagery and context. Try to hear the voice of this man telling you his life story with the intensity that comes only from one who has personally lived the experience.

Jesse D. Fuller

Chapter 1
El Salvador

My story begins in El Carmen, Usulutan, Jurisdiction of Jiquilisco, El Salvador. My father, Carlos Mejia Guerrero, was just seven years old when his father died, leaving behind four children. Eduardo, one of his brothers, died from an unknown illness. Isabel, his other brother, was killed by a drunk man. My father's mother, Herminia, was remarried to Sebastian Chavez and they gave birth to four more children. After my grandmother gave birth to her last child, she died. Not too long after my grandmother's death, Sebastian abandoned them, leaving my father and his sister, Juana, responsible for their three half brothers and half sister.

The only skill my father ever had, and has even now, is farming. To survive, he would plant small plots here and there to provide some food during the growing seasons for his brothers and sisters. They also were forced to go into the streets and beg for food, clothing, and shelter from place to place. While out on the streets begging with his brothers and sisters, my father met the woman who would later become my mother, Paula Elvira Lopez.

For them to establish a relationship was not easy, because she was grieving the loss of her own father, who had passed away not too long before they met. An even bigger obstacle was my father's responsibility for his brothers and sisters, one she would have to share. Somehow she accepted the challenge and they were married. My father was 20 years old and my mother was 16.

While they were still dating, my dad had built a bajareque,(ba ha reckē) house for his brothers and sisters, so this was where he took his new wife to live with them. A bajareque is a simple hut that consisted of one large room with no electricity or running water. Bajareque comes from the Nahualt(na walt) Indians and means mud-filled bars. Wooden poles were driven vertically into the ground in the shape of the hut. Wood bars were tied onto the inside and outside of the poles horizontally with bejuco(bā hookō) vines at three-inch intervals from the bottom to the top of the poles. Then the spaces were filled from the top with mud that was sometimes mixed with grasses. The roof was more poles tied together at the top like a teepee with more horizontal bars and grasses tied to it. The hut had a dirt floor.

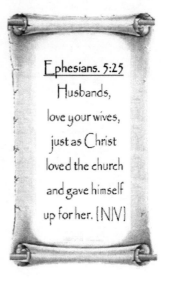

Ephesians. 5:25

Husbands, love your wives, just as Christ loved the church and gave himself up for her. [NIV]

Their life wasn't easy. Two weeks after their wedding, one of my father's brothers was playing with firecrackers and set the house on fire. The fire destroyed the few things they had. This was another of many life struggles for the young couple. Even so, my father gave his wife all his love and whatever other things he could possibly provide for her.

After the fire, my father moved his family to a piece of property owned by a woman they called "Ticha" (Tee cha). There my parents built the bajareque where their children would be raised. Twenty-five or thirty other poor families also lived on this property. There was a large hacienda with stables there where the administrators who worked for Ticha lived and where Ticha would stay when she visited. For at least one month of the year, my father worked for Ticha helping to maintain her property as payment for the use of the land on which my dad had built our hut.

On January 8, 1971, I was born, José Medardo Mejia. I was the sixth of their eleven children: Herminia, Pedro, Arturo, Catalina, Jilma, me, Cristabel, Lorena, Vitelia, Sylvia, and Arturo Jr. And this is **my** story.

Walking by a Miracle!

As I said earlier, my dad was a farmer. The produce he grew not only fed our family, it was also used to trade for things we needed and to provide a small income. Since he did not own any land, he also used the produce to trade for the use of the land he farmed and the rental of oxen used to pull the plow.

In April of 1972, I developed symptoms of typhoid fever and polio. This was the mark of the beginning of my suffering and the beginning of God's

Victory!
The Life of José M. Mejia

Grace over my life. In August of 1972, the doctors confirmed that I indeed did have these two illnesses, typhoid fever and polio. That month, I was hospitalized as an intensive care patient at Benjamin Bloom Children's Hospital in San Salvador, El Salvador. This was an extreme hardship for my parents. At the time, they had five children older than me and one younger. Their income was the lowest in the country. The hospital was about 120 miles from their home. They had to walk about 20 miles to the highway where they could take a bus the remaining 100 miles to the hospital. My parents would try to come to see me at least once a month because they could not afford to come more often. The love they had for each other and for their children was all that got them through this difficult time.

To pay for the expenses of my hospitalization and the cost of transportation, my parents began to sell anything that was in good enough condition to be sold. After everything had been sold, they went to their friends to borrow money. They thought that my illness would last only for a month or two, but to their surprise, the doctors told them that if I was lucky enough to survive the illnesses, I would still suffer with the effects of them for the rest of my life.

As time passed, my parents sold or lost everything they had. But one thing they didn't lose was their hope and love for me. They sacrificed themselves until they were so low they touched the ground. After three years of being in the intensive care unit at the children's hospital, I was finally released. The doctors gave my parents no hope that I would ever become a normal boy. The left side of my body was completely paralyzed from the top of my head to the bottom of my foot. I was almost five years old and weighed less than twenty pounds. Even though my parents had carried me home, they had to keep returning to the hospital with me every two weeks for therapy. My parents were at a loss as to what to do with me or what to give me that might improve my health. The doctors did not prescribe any medication for me, which made the situation for my parents even worse. In their desperation, my parents began to rub my body and joints with all kinds of plants that were growing around us in the nearby jungle. They tried everything to help me.

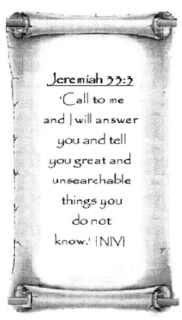

Jeremiah 33:3

'Call to me and I will answer you and tell you great and unsearchable things you do not know.' [NIV]

My parents were faithful in getting me to the hospital for my therapy and during one of those journeys, in May of 1976, someone gave me an apple. When we arrived at the hospital, the doctor began my routine examination. My mother put my apple aside.

One of the assistant nurses saw my apple and said, "That apple looks delicious! I am going to eat it!"

I exclaimed, "That's my apple!" I jumped up from the stretcher and went to grab my apple. What a tremendous surprise that was for my mother and the hospital personnel, as well as for me!

Victory!
The Life of José M. Mejia

On that very day, God renewed my bones and all the tissues in my body. He healed me completely. From that day on, I began to walk. This miracle was kept in my mother's mind for the rest of her life. Many times when I was playing, running or climbing a tree, she used to come and hug me.

She would say, "Son, many times when I see you walking or doing all that you do, it is incomprehensible and unbelievable what you can do."

I used to ask my mom, "Why?"

To answer my question, she just started relating my life story and how she saw me walk. It was impossible for her not to cry when she was telling the story, which made me cry, too.

Exodus 15:26

...for I am the Lord, who heals you.

(NIV)

Recently, I met my father's old friend who I had never met before. He was introduced to me by my cousin and told me a story I had never heard. When this man saw me he got a big surprise and said, "So you are Carlos Mejia's son?"

"Yes, I am," I replied.

"The last time I saw you, you were about five years old and your dad had you in a hole. He had covered half of your body with warm dirt. He thought the warmth of the earth would help strengthen your body. I never thought you would be healed," he exclaimed.

He told me he had walked away from the Lord many years ago, but now after seeing what the Lord had done for me, he rededicated himself to the Lord right there.

Let me tell you, my friend, God is real! God exists! In Mark 10:27 Jesus says, "... With men it is impossible, but not with God: for with God all things are possible." {KJV} When man says there is no hope, Jesus tells us He is our hope. Jesus said, "I am the way, the truth, and the life:..." John 14:6 {KJV} Twenty years later, I understood the meaning of this verse and how it impacted my life. The three main words in this verse (**way, truth, and life**) were taking place in my life, one at a time, without my knowledge because I didn't know God's word. The doctors sent me home saying that there was no cure for me. At that moment God gave me **life** to prove to all mankind that He is the Giver of Life because I didn't die when, by man's standards, I should have died. Since then, I can see that God's word **"life"** took place inside of me.

If you do not know the God I am talking about, I invite you to open the door of your heart and ask God to dwell in it. Or perhaps you know but have walked away from Him. I invite you to return to Him. You will see how sweet is our God.

Chapter 2

Invasion

In 1976, prior to my healing, my father began to build a house. He worked on the house for over a year and finished it in May of 1977. This house was our first normal house. I say normal because we had been living in huts. This house had three rooms used for bedrooms and living areas while the kitchen still remained outside. We still had no indoor plumbing or electricity.

In early 1978, the political problems began in my country of El Salvador. There were manifestations all over the country, with poor people pitted against the government and wealthy people. The wealthy people owned the country. Because of their wealth and economic power, the government supported them, doing whatever they wanted.

Abusing their power, the wealthy authorized their guards to kill the poor people when they came to ask for their wages or for help with living expenses. Because of these increasingly intolerable conditions, the poor finally rebelled. They stopped working in the fields and gathered in common areas in protest against the wealthy land owners treatment of them. This rebellion incited outbreaks of violence.

Victory!
The Life of José M. Mejia

The government sent the army to try to stop these uprisings between the wealthy and poor, but that only led to an increase in the violence resulting in a civil war. A few months later, the poor began forming armed rebel groups to fight against the wealthy people and the government. By 1979, the rebel groups were strongly armed with heavy-duty weapons they had obtained with the help of other countries or from soldiers they had killed.

Unfortunately for us, the armed rebel groups had established their main camp sites in our village. They forced all the people in the village to integrate into their group. My father was forced to collaborate with these guerilla troops. As I remember, I was just seven years old and the guerrillas used to take me and other children of the village to pose for pictures with weapons hung on us. I am not sure of the purpose of those pictures, but many used to say they were used to make fliers to advertise the strength of the rebel forces and intimidate the army and rich people.

For the rebels, age and gender were not an issue. They forced everyone to join their forces or do something to support the group. There were just two ways, join them and live or refuse and die. My older brother, Pedro, like so many others, had been forced to join the guerilla forces. At age 17, he had to leave our family and go off to fight with the guerillas.

The government "red tagged" several areas of at least 20 small towns and villages, including our village. Anyone who had documents showing they lived in a red-tagged area, past or present, was deemed by the government to be a rebel and killed, no questions asked.

In 1979, the war had escalated. The rebels were bombing public buildings, bridges, power lines, and private businesses. The government was building a stronger army. In December of 1979, the government army invaded our "red zone" for the first time. They killed many, many civilians, mostly women and children. When my parents would hear that the army was near, they would flee with us and the other villagers to avoid being killed. We hid in the jungle, sleeping in caves or just under the trees, eating whatever we could find around us. Even in this frightening time, I can remember the beautiful things of our land like "Cueva Pintada" (Cave of Colors) with it's brilliant colors caused by water running into the cave. These times in the jungle would last sometimes for a week or more. We would return to our home only when the fighting subsided.

Because we were from what was considered a rebel area, it was impossible for us to go to the city to buy anything. The army stationed troops at all the entrances to our area. Anyone attempting to enter or leave was killed. One morning, my cousin, Angel, was captured by the army on his way to the city. They cut his head off and hung it on a fence post, leaving his body about a quarter of a mile away. The same thing happened to my uncles and to many other people I knew.

On December 10, 1980, my older brother, Arturo, was killed by the army. He was going to town to buy medicine for my mother. The army saw him coming from the red zone and tried to catch him. My brother knew that if they caught him he would be killed, cut apart piece by piece. He decided to run away. As he ran, a soldier shot him with a machine gun. We did not see him or bury him because the army kept his body to see if anyone would come to pick him up. If someone did, they would do the same thing to them as they did to my brother. A friend of ours who lived in the city had some connection with the soldiers. He was able to see my brother's body, but he did not tell the soldiers he knew my brother because they would have killed him, also. This friend told us that my brother had nearly one hundred bullet holes in his body. He was just 15 years old.

In February of 1981, the army invaded our village again. The rebels always posted guards at many points to watch for any army movements. After several months of upheaval, we heard the rebels' signal bombs exploding at approximately 6:00 one morning. This signal meant that the army was coming into the village, and everyone was forced to flee, because there was no chance of survival in the hands of the army soldiers. Again, my family fled our home. My sister, Lorena, was sick. My mother could not walk quickly or for long distances because she was pregnant, so finally she stopped and said to my dad, "Carlos, I can not flee anymore! Please, run away with our older daughters. I am going to return home with the younger children. Maybe the soldiers will have mercy and let us live."

So my father told Herminia, Catalina, and Jilma to stay there and wait for him. He helped my mother get the younger children back home. He barely had time to set the children on our porch before he had to rush away to avoid the nearby fighting. He returned to where his daughters were waiting and continued fleeing with them.

My mother took Lorena, Crista, Vitelia, Sylvia, and me back into the house. There were many other families fleeing at this time and we were the only ones left in our village.

The soldiers were burning all the fields in the area, trapping a large number of people from several of the villages in the red zone, including my father and sisters. At one point, the soldiers had two fires burning towards each other, one on either side of the group my father was with. There were not too many ways to escape. They were trapped between the fires. The whole group was confused and strangling on the heavy smoke. Groups of people were scattering in different directions. Most of them just ran into the lion's mouth, into the hands of the army. The soldiers began shooting into the crowds of villagers; men, women, and children. People fell to the ground trying to hide from the bullets. In one of those groups was my father's sister, Aunt Juana, who was killed there. My sister, Herminia was on the ground next to three people that were killed by the soldiers' bullets. The army killed at least 75 to 100 people there that day. The people that they captured alive were tortured brutally before being killed.

Scared and wanting to protect his children, my father decided to leave the group. As he and my sisters dashed back toward

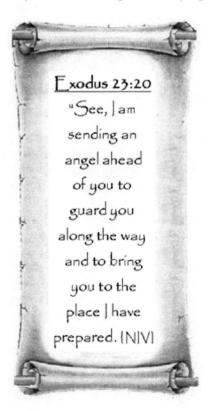

Exodus 23:20

"See, I am sending an angel ahead of you to guard you along the way and to bring you to the place I have prepared. (NIV)

the river, the rest of the group was killed by fire, bombs, or bullets. As he approached the river with his daughters, they saw many soldiers coming toward them. They were only about five yards away. They stopped and waited, but the soldiers did not see them and turned down another path. They were able to escape into the forest to hide. The weight on my father's shoulders was great. His worry for his wife was terrible because there were fires all around them. He could tell that the fighting and bombardment was in the direction of our house. There was no chance for him to go to our house or even get close to it. Leaving part of his family behind was an indescribable torture for him. It put him between the rock and the sword, especially when the fighting was so close. All he could do was wait for the fighting to subside, so he could go to find the rest of his family.

From our house, we could hear the fighting between the army and the rebels getting closer. We were huddled together under a bed or table or some piece of furniture, crying and clinging to our mother. Even though it was summer and the temperature was in excess of 100°F, we were choking and felt cold because of the extreme state of panic we were in. My mother was very frightened and did not know what to do to help or comfort us. The only solution she could think of was that we should all commit suicide, thinking perhaps that would be more peaceful than the nightmare we were experiencing.

At approximately 1:00 p.m., a soldier came to our house. Seeing a soldier that close was like looking into the face of death. When many more soldiers entered our home, they immediately put us all on the ground, holding their guns over our heads. They began to mistreat our mother, insulting her and asking her about my father and the guerillas. They accused her of being an accomplice of the guerillas, too. When my mother didn't answer their questions, they grabbed her by the hair and dragged her outside to kill her. A soldier put his gun to her forehead and said, "Say goodbye to your life." My four sisters and I were surrounding our screaming mother, clinging to each other, grabbing at her skirt. We were crying and pleading with the soldiers who were mistreating her. We cried out, "Please, don't kill our mother. If you must kill her, please kill us, too." The soldier just pushed us aside and kept kicking my mother's knees. Finally, he told her that if she would not talk to them, she must cook for them. The soldiers killed our chickens and forced my mother to cook them along with our store of corn, beans, and rice. She cooked for them all night long and for the next two days as more soldiers circulated through our village and the rest of the red zone, looking for the guerillas. Even though we were not allowed to eat, my mother was able to get small amounts of food to us, a few bits of tortillas, as we huddled close by watching her work.

After the army had occupied our home for three days, the guerillas attacked them in our house. The fighting began in the morning and lasted all day long and into the night. We saw and heard hundreds of bullets flying through the house. Again, we found ourselves huddled together in a corner of our home as broken pieces of tile fell everywhere. Grenades were exploding all around us. Dead and wounded soldiers were lying all around in the house and on the patio. My sisters' noses and ears were bleeding from the concussion of exploding bombs. Even though the soldiers saw my sisters bleeding, they couldn't care less about them. They considered us worse than the dogs that were lying with us on the dirt floor.

Victory!
The Life of José M. Mejia

The next morning the soldiers moved their wounded to Ticha's hacienda, about three hundred yards away. A helicopter came in and hovered over the hacienda to pick up the wounded soldiers. The guerillas had moved into the trees near our house to hide until they could attack the soldiers again. As the helicopter was lifting off, the guerillas attacked, moving out of the trees in front of our house. This time the soldiers fled.

All we could do is huddle together in fear inside our house and wait to see what would happen next. Later that day, two army planes came to bomb the area. They dropped five bombs near our house.

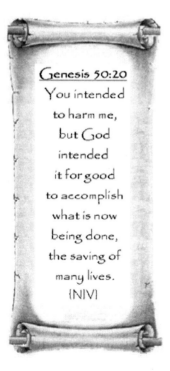

Genesis 50:20

You intended

to harm me,

but God

intended

it for good

to accomplish

what is now

being done,

the saving of

many lives.

(NIV)

Four of them fell about a quarter mile away. The fifth bomb landed within 60 feet. We were in the house at the time, but the bomb did not explode. It was faulty. It didn't explode because God protected us. God is the only reason that bomb did not blow up.

After the bombing, the soldiers returned. They took us out of our house, gathering everything that was in it. Then they set the house on fire. They just burned our home and left us there with no shelter. There was not a single home standing in the area. All of them were destroyed. Everywhere we looked we saw dead bodies. We had nothing to eat or to cover ourselves with. Our only covering was Heaven itself. There is a Salvadorian song that suddenly made sense to me, "The Salvadorian people have the blue sky as their hat."

We were all alone. We didn't know if our father and sisters had survived the fighting. We had not seen or heard from Pedro in over three months. We did not know where he was or if he was alive. My mother didn't know what to do. She felt the need to stay there in hopes of the rest of her family returning. We survived by sleeping under the trees and eating wild fruit, edible leaves, and roots. We spent our days hiding among the trees, avoiding any contact with the army forces, trying not to be seen by the many planes and helicopters flying over the area looking for guerillas.

A few weeks later, some people began to appear, coming back to the village. They were so malnourished it appeared that the only thing holding their bones together was their skin. We asked if they had seen our father and sisters, but they had not. We stayed near the village area, surviving day to day, waiting for any word from the rest of our family.

The invasion lasted for more than a month; and during this time, my father and sisters faced death over and over. The energy of their bodies was nearly gone. My father knew that people were being killed in the larger groups and it was easier to hide with just a few people, so he and my sisters traveled alone. The guerillas did provide some food to those groups, every other day or so, but still, my father felt he could protect his daughters better away from those groups. In spite of the weather and starvation, he was relieved to have his daughters by his side. He knew he would do even the impossible to protect them. His suffering was enormous, but worst of all was the worry of having left his wife and other children behind. Sometimes my sisters fainted from starvation and the worry about their mother and siblings.

Days later, when the attack had ceased, little by little they tried to get back home. When the fighting moved out of the area where our house was located, they began to make the journey back to our village. As they walked they saw pregnant women with their stomachs cut wide open and their babies pulled out from their wombs. It was not clear if they were killed before or after this terrible mutilation. Other people were hanging on stakes or had stakes in their behinds and eyes. Some had their genitals cut off and shoved into their mouths. Miraculously, my father and sisters had run away in different directions from the large groups. That is the only reason they survived the soldier's senseless tortures and mutilations during this brutal massacre.

Reunited

Finally, they got to the house where they had left us. When they saw it, they went into a state of shock. Our house was gone! There was not a single sign of life. The anguish that my father's soul felt at that very moment was indescribable. There were no more tears left in his eyes or his daughters' eyes. My sisters just fainted away and Dad could only sob with a force that was wracking his lungs.

Victory!
The Life of José M. Mejia

Seeing them lying on the ground, he thought that he had lost his daughters, too. He didn't know what to do anymore. He didn't have even the strength to see if they were breathing. Minutes later, they recovered.

They went to survey the ashes of the house to see if they could find any evidence of us, but found nothing. While my father felt relief that we had not been killed in the house fire, his hope of finding us alive diminished. They walked away and kept looking for us. Sometime later, they were walking by the thick woods where we were hiding. That's when I saw Dad for the first time since the invasion.

"Dad! Dad! Dad!" I cried. He turned and saw me, his little José, running toward him. Their spirits came back to them as they started running to me. Dad lifted me up and hugged me tightly, as did my sisters.

He then asked me, "Where are your mom and sisters?"

I pointed and said, "They are right there, under those trees."

My father said that when he saw me he felt like he was having a dream. It was unbelievable what he was hearing and seeing: we were alive! We were so dirty, he told us that we looked like we had been working in a charcoal factory.

What a wonderful gift! Our family was almost complete again. We all cried out to Heaven together.

In my introduction I told you that my dad said, "There is no doubt that there is someone or something above all human beings." I glorify God and honor Him because that "something" that my dad talked about is God. God that is in Heaven, and not just in Heaven, was protecting my father and sisters. He's the One who stopped the bullets that did not kill my dad and sisters. He's the One who made the soldiers blind and caused them to take another trail so they didn't see my dad and sisters.

Let me tell you, my brother, sister, or friend, that even though all of this is over, right now as I am sharing the story of my life with you, I am weeping, because my wounds are opened once again. Wounds that bring back the memories of all those moments that destroyed the lives of so many of my relatives and left an everlasting scar on my life. One thing I do not do is complain about those days because now I can see that God was watching over me. Remembering my past brings much pain deep in my heart, but now that I am a strong believer in Jesus Christ, His Power, His Love, and His Mercy, my courage is fortified. I continue serving the Lord, my Savior, with a desire to increase His Kingdom and snatch the souls that satan has captivated with his lies in the darkness of the

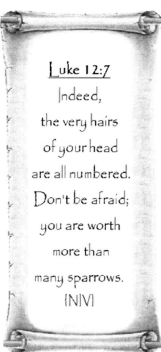

Luke 12:7

Indeed,

the very hairs

of your head

are all numbered.

Don't be afraid;

you are worth

more than

many sparrows.

(NIV)

world. This liar (satan) has to know that we have a
Holy Father in Heaven that is watching over us and
He has promised He knows the number of hairs on
our head and we are worth more than anything to
Him.

For me without a doubt, God's protection is
always there, even though we haven't yet cried out to
Him.

Chapter 3
Survival

My father and sisters were even skinnier than the other villagers had been. Now our chances to escape from the area were even less than before the invasion. Because of our poor physical condition, anyone would recognize we were from the red zone. So my father began to build a shelter hut just two miles from our old house. While he worked on the hut, the rest of us went around the area to find household things we could use to help us survive. We found things like pots and cooking items. We also found plants with gourd-like fruit and used them to make huacal(wa kal', meaning bowls).

The need for basic products was enormous. We had lost everything when the house burned. There was no chance for us to go town to get any supplies, such as sugar, salt, soap, corn, etc. because trying to go to town was as to offer our life to death. We had to try to live with just those things and food we could find around us.

One day a memory flashed in my mother's mind. She cried out to my dad, "The corn, Carlos! The corn!"

Confused, my dad asked, "What corn?"

She replied, "The corn that we have buried under the old house. Maybe it didn't burn up."

In the middle of our great starvation and after all the anguish that we had been through, we had all forgotten that about three months before the big invasion we helped my dad dig a huge hole in one of the porches of the house. There he had buried a 6' by 10' metal container that he filled about half full of corn. The memory returned to my dad and he jumped up from the log where he was sitting and shouted, "That's true!"

It was about 2 p.m. and the day was very hot, but we all rushed to the remains of the old house and started cleaning up the area where my dad had buried the container of corn. With the help of my mother and older sisters, he dug the hole again. The container of corn was there, untouched. When we saw this, my sisters and I just grabbed each other's hands and danced in circles, saying, "Corn! Corn! We have corn!" My mother and my dad just sat on the ground with their feet in the hole and cried. We took what was necessary for two weeks and buried the container again. We went back to the shelter that dad had built, carrying the corn and the happiness that we had from finding it.

To cook corn for tortillas, my mother used to use lime. She would boil the corn in water with lime to cause the peels to come off

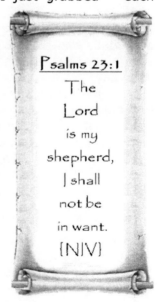

Psalms 23:1

The
Lord
is my
shepherd,
I shall
not be
in want.

(NIV)

the corn. She would then wash the corn to remove the lime and peels and grind the rest into masa. Because we didn't have any lime for her to prepare the corn we found, my mother used ashes to peel the corn. My dad then washed just enough of the boiled corn that we would eat in our next meal. He left the rest of the corn in the ash water to preserve it. My mother ground the cleaned corn on the metatae or piedra de moler. Metatae is a flat rock about 20 inches long by 18 inches wide and about 3 inches thick. A round rock about 4 inches thick by ten inches long was used to grind the corn against the metatae. For the first time in many weeks we were going to eat tortillas again!

As time passed, my parents tried to re-establish a home for us, little by little. The ash that my mother was using was not good enough for the corn to be peeled completely. For that she needed lime. We didn't have any salt, sugar, oil, or beans, either; just the corn we found, the animals we caught and some wild fruit. But, we were all very happy to eat just tortillas and meat from wild animals everyday.

One day I asked my dad if he would let me try to sneak into town to see if I could buy some products that we needed. He didn't like that idea one bit. Later on, I asked him again.

He told me, "With what money are we going to buy such things, son? We do not have any pisto!" Pisto is a slang word use by people on the east side of El Salvador to mean "cash."

To this I said, "Dad, maybe I can take some of the corn we have hidden and sell or trade it for salt, sugar, oil, and lime."

He just stayed silent. But I just kept insisting.

Finally, he said, "Son, it's just too dangerous to go to town. You know that!"

"Yes," I said, "but if the soldiers catch me I will tell them that all my family died in the invasion and maybe they would let me go."

He told my mom about my idea and she didn't agree either. But I kept on insisting and finally they agreed to let me go.

We filled a bag with all the corn that I could carry, only about 25 pounds, maybe less. By the time I left it was already after noon. My dad went with me as far as he could safely go and then I went the rest of the way myself. After I left my dad, I thought I was going alone, but now that I understand the love and caring of God for me and my family, I can see that I was not walking alone. God was guarding me. I didn't see a single person or soldier until I got to town.

I went to a little market and told the woman that was attending the store that I wanted to trade the corn that I was carrying for sugar, salt, oil, lime, and beans.

She said, "I'm sorry boy, but I can not do that. Besides that, the corn that you are carrying is not enough to pay for all that you want."

I said to her, "Please, can you help me? I am tired of carrying this corn already."

She asked me, "Where are you coming from?"

I almost cried when she asked me this question. My mind flashed to Arturo's brutal death. I was afraid that if she knew where I was coming from, she might try to detain me and turn me over to the Army forces which would mean my death, also. I just avoided her questions and with tears in my eyes, I pleaded again, "Please! Can you help me?"

She wiped her eyes and I could see she was crying, too. I knew she understood our great need and the risk I took in coming there. She said, "Okay I will help you." She took the bag of corn and went into the store and dumped it into another sack. She put some stuff in the bag I was carrying and said, "Here, son. Please, be careful wherever you are going!" I thanked her very much and left the store.

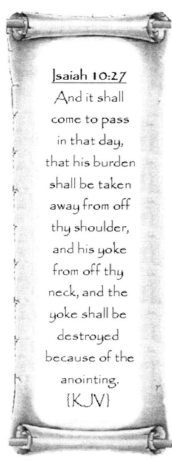

Isaiah 10:27

And it shall come to pass in that day, that his burden shall be taken away from off thy shoulder, and his yoke from off thy neck, and the yoke shall be destroyed because of the anointing.

{KJV}

I had to walk at least three hours to get to the place where my dad left me. I was walking as fast as I could. It was getting late and I felt the way back home was longer than when I came, maybe because I was tired and had a lot of fear. I kept walking and walking. Finally, not too far from the place where my dad had left me, I saw him waiting for me. I felt a little relief.

"I was worried about you!" he said.

He grabbed the bag I was carrying and put me on his back and carried me for awhile. In the meantime, I was telling him what had happened on the way to the store and about

33

the woman that bought the corn.

Doubtfully, he said, "Son, that woman gave you more than the value of the corn that you took."

To that I replied, "That's what she said, but she didn't say anything else and gave me all these things."

Night fell before we got home. When we were getting close to the house, I saw a very tiny light coming through the holes of our shack and I told my dad, maybe Mom is still awake.

To this he replied, "Your mom has been worried about you. She even wanted to go to town to look for you, but I didn't let her go."

To that I couldn't answer anything. Tears just rolled over my cheeks. Thinking of what could have happened to my mother if she had come to look for me was very painful. That decision could have cost my mother's life.

When we got home, we didn't want to scare my mom, so we tried to be as quiet as we could. My dad went to one of the holes of the shack and called my mom to open the door. She didn't pay too much attention to what we were bringing. She just hugged me and said, "Son, you are going to give me a heart attack!"

I couldn't say anything about that. And then I said, "Look, Mom, at what we are bringing."

She grabbed the bag and said, "Son, this was too heavy for you."

I said, "No, Mom! The corn was heavier than this."

"No, son." she replied. "The corn was not much heavier. Was it, Carlos?", she said, looking at my dad.

When my sisters heard us talking, they got up. They were saying, "José! Dad!" They wanted to see

Phil 4:19
And my
God
will meet all
your needs
according
to his
glorious riches
in
Christ
Jesus.
(NIV)

what was in the bag. My mother just opened the bag and put some sugar on their hands. They giggled and began to lick their hands. My mom fed Dad and me with the tortillas that she had already made and some fish that she had cooked on the comal, our cooking pan. Because we didn't have any dishes, she just put the fish on the tortillas and spread a little salt from what we just brought her. We were all at that moment so glad to be together, feeling life would be okay.

Maybe you will think that I am crazy, but as I am writing I can not stop glorifying God and saying Hallelujah, God is good! He is good! My tears are unstoppable at this very moment, just to see how faithful is my God. I don't know if your God is that faithful, but if you don't have a god such as the One I have, that sent His only Son, Jesus, to die for us and to **supply for all our needs.** I recommend Him to you, my friend. I just bend my knees before my God and Jesus Christ, Giver of Life, because He's the only One that keeps our life in His hands.

Chapter 4

Escape

At the end of 1981, I was nearly eleven years old and we finally had news about Pedro, my older brother who had been forced to join the guerillas nearly two years before. He was alive. That's all we knew.

During this quieter time of fighting, my parents tried to decide what to do next. The living situation in the area was growing worse. Because of her pregnant condition, my father felt it would be best for my mother to take the children and escape the red zone without him. The reason he did not try to escape with us was because there were many people that had left the zone and now were involved with the army. Their job was to point out all the people that they knew from the red zone. The people they pointed out would then be killed. There were army checkpoints everywhere, where the soldiers were taking people from the buses to be killed. One of those checkpoints was where we would have to pass to escape to the city. This checkpoint was at the bridge called El Puente de Oro, the Bridge of Gold. It was one of the most cruel checkpoints.

Victory!
The Life of José M. Mejia

So my father sent us away to escape the fighting. We walked the twenty miles to the highway and took the bus to the city, leaving my father behind to flee alone. My two older sisters went to live with my uncle who lived in Zacatecoluca. My mother, younger sisters, and I went to live with my mother's sister who lived about 100 miles away from the red zone in Cojutepeque. We had nothing to take on the journey, just ten pounds of salt and our sick bodies.

During the weeks at my aunt's house, we were mistreated so horribly that I felt I had been more at peace under the bullets. We used our aunt's house only for a place to stay at night. During the day, we went from one market to another begging for food. Sometimes we went to hospitals to get shelter from the rains or to swap meets to try to beg for food. When we weren't out begging, we would spend our days sitting under a tree if there was no rain. I recall on those days how my mother would make coffee by grinding burnt, leftover tortillas. Even though we were out of the red zone and living with relatives, we were all still very malnourished. We longed to be with our dad again.

Even though it was dangerous, several times, my mother would allow me to try to go to the red zone to see if I could find Dad. But it was impossible. To get there, it was necessary for me to sneak onto a bus. During this time of fighting, the guerillas were stopping the buses at gunpoint. All the people would be taken off the bus and made to hand over their money. Then the guerillas would burn the bus. Other times, the buses could not make it through because the bridges were broken down or the soldiers would stop them at their checkpoints because it was too dangerous for them to go through.

Victory!
The Life of José M. Mejia

Although most of the trains had been burned during the fighting, by this time a few of the trains were working again in some areas. On one occasion, I hopped on a train to try to go find my dad. Most of the time there were soldiers on the trains to protect them. When the train I was on began crossing a bridge called Puente del Burro in San Vincente, the Donkey Bridge, the guerrilla attacked. The train didn't stop. The soldiers were shooting their guns from the train cars. In the car where I was, two people were killed and even more in the other cars. It was impossible for me to go to find my dad that day. I took another train back to my aunt's place. I didn't tell my mom about what had happened because I knew she would never let me go again.

On June 16, 1982, my mother took us to a creek about a mile away from our aunt's house to do laundry. While my mother was bending over the creek, she felt the beginning pains of childbirth. She left us at the creek and returned to our aunt's house. After she left us, my sisters and I finished washing the laundry. Sylvia, who was about two years old at the time, was very sick, so Cristabel, Jilma, Vitelia, Lorena, and I carried her, along with all the wet laundry, back to our aunt's house. When we arrived there, we learned that our mother barely made it to the house where a neighbor and my aunt helped her deliver my youngest brother. She told us that our brother would be called Arturo after our older brother who had been killed by the soldiers.

During the next month, Sylvia's illness grew even worse. I was the oldest one with them besides my sister, Jilma, and Mother. I told my mother I wanted to go and see if I could find my father again to tell him about what was happening with Sylvia.

Victory!
The Life of José M. Mejía

The war was continuing, increasing in strength. The dangers were even worse than before. My dad was surviving by wandering from place to place with some relatives and friends that were in the same situation as him. Tired of constantly fleeing, they returned to their huts in the village. For protection, they dug a large cave by the riverside where at least 20 people could be hidden when the troops were in the area. They would sometimes have to spend many days in the cave. They went out at night only to make some tortillas with corn or other things such as dried fish or meat that they kept underground. While some people were outside the cave cooking, others were watching for any danger.

So I left the city to find him. I was only eleven years old or so, but somehow I sneaked onto a bus without paying because I had not a single cent in my pocket. When the bus got to a place closest to the red zone, I got off and began to walk to where I thought my father would be, about 20 miles from where the bus left me. One thing I noticed was that all the while I was walking it was so quiet. Only once in awhile would I hear a bomb explode or the noise of a gunshot. I finally arrived at the village area, but my father wasn't there. I couldn't stop thinking of a worse tragedy than possibly finding that my dad was dead. That's all I could think about. I sat there for awhile just thinking about my mother and sisters. There was no one around. After awhile I opened the door of the hut my father had built for us and found fresh food there. This gave me hope and brought my spirit back to me.

After an hour more of waiting, my father finally returned. When I saw him coming, I ran into his arms and clung to him. We didn't say a single word. We just hugged and cried out loud.

My father had been to the river to do his laundry and to try to catch some fish. While, he was there, he saw some people fleeing because the army was coming up to the zone. He rushed back to his place to get the food that he had already cooked to take with him. That's when he saw me waiting for him.

As I reflect back on this scene, I am amazed to think about what could possibly have made him go back to the hut where he found me instead of fleeing with the group at the river. His natural instinct had always been to flee immediately, to think of nothing else but getting away from the army. Even though the moment we had was very brief, I can see now it had been God working on our side.

He told me, "Son, I am happy to see you, but we are in great danger. The army is already in the area and I have only two choices, son, to flee or let them catch me."

I told him, "No, dad. Don't let them catch you. I'm going back to where my mother is. Please run away."

He said, "I think it is too late for you to get out of here. More soldiers are coming. If they find you walking, I don't know what they might do to you." Pointing, he said, "In those houses are some older people with their grandsons. Go and stay with them."

I told him, "Dad, before you go, I came here just to tell you that my sister, Sylvia, is dying."

He just bowed his head and cried more. He was silent for awhile, then he said, "I am sorry, son. There is nothing I can do at this very moment."

Until that moment when he found me there sitting on a rock outside his hut door, his heart had been broken. His joy was mixed with anguish and desperation. To hear that his wife and other children were safe where they were gave him relief, but the news that I brought about Sylvia's illness was painful because there was nothing he could do to help her. His only choice was to send me to a place where he thought I would be safe until the soldiers left the area again.

We hugged each other again and I went where he told me to go. He fled, also.

It was almost too late for my father to get away. Then only five minutes after I arrived at that house, the soldiers arrived. They dragged everyone out of the house and without asking very many questions, they began to mistreat us. They beat the older men and women. One sergeant said to one of the soldiers, "You are the one who will kill all these people." They put us in a line and the sergeant told the soldier, "When I give the order, kill all of them." He began counting from one to ten before giving the killing order. At that moment, another sergeant came along. "What are you doing?" he asked. The first sergeant answered, "These people don't

Ps 71:4

Deliver me, O my God, from the hand of the wicked, from the grasp of evil and cruel men.

(NIV)

want to talk, so I am going to kill them!" The second sergeant replied, "We are not going to kill innocent people. Leave these people alone." They finally released us, but not before raping all the women, killing two of them.

After this confrontation with the army, I stayed with these people for two more days, hoping to see my dad one more time before I left. But that was impossible, so I decided to try to go back to where my mother and sisters were. It was dangerous to walk anywhere because there were underground bombs that had killed many people and children. Many had lost legs or arms to these bombs. I risked my life and walked back to the highway to catch a bus. There were no vehicles on the road. The highway had been closed because most of the bridges had been blown up during the bombings. So I continued walking. Most of the houses along the way were empty, but I finally found some houses where people were living. Even though I didn't know these people, they let me stay with them for three days. I set out walking along the highway again until I found a place where vehicles would occasionally pass. One of them picked me up and took me to where I was able to take a bus.

I finally arrived back where my mother was staying. Sadly, Sylvia had died two days prior. This news was so painful to me that I became sick.

We stayed at my aunt's house until nearly the end of 1982 when an uncle from my father's side found us. When he saw the condition in which we were living, he said, "I do not have much to offer you but where I live, I will be able to find a better place than this. I am working on a ranch where we will have a better opportunity." He left then and returned a week later and took us back with him. God bless my Uncle Luis.

Chapter 5
The Ranch

The ranch where Uncle Luis was working was located along side the highway that goes from San Salvador to the International Airport of Comalapa. The Salvadorean authorities had formed a group named El Escuadron de la Muerte, the Death Squadron. Their job was just to randomly kill people, guilty or not. Every morning on the ranch land we found at least ten dead people that the squadron had killed the night before. They were just thrown out there without their heads. Before going to work in the fields each morning, the ranch workers had to bury those dead people.

There on the ranch was an empty old house that Uncle Luis told us to move into. For the first time in my life, I felt a little peace in my heart. I felt that I was in a real home, except that my family was not yet complete. My father was not there with us. One brother and one sister had died. My other two sisters were far away from us and we didn't know where my older brother was. But on the other hand, I was comforted by the fact that my mother was safer there on the ranch.

We worked together to make this place our home. We cleaned up the area around the house, gathered firewood and food, and built a cooking area for my mother—just little things to feel like we were living again. I would also help my uncle in the fields.

Finding My Father

About six months later, my mother went to look for my father. She found him and he was able to leave the red zone this time and come home with her. I will never forget that day. Mom had been gone for almost a week. It was almost dark when I saw a very skinny man walking by my mother's side. I didn't recognize him at first because he was wearing very ragged clothing and an old stained hat. That was the best gift I ever received from God, except for receiving His gift of Jesus. What a gift, to see my dad again!

I would like to say something here to you, my brother, sister, or friend, as you are reading this testimony. Appreciate the gifts that God has given to you. If you have a mother or father or both that are still alive, love them with all your heart. Give all the flowers that you can, now while they can smell the sweet aromas because after death the flowers will have no more aroma for them.

When I realized it was my dad, I ran to him, wanting to tell him everything at once. My sisters did the same thing. We clung to each other and cried for a while then we took him into the house. We showed him where we were living with no more soldiers or rebels around us.

He was very sick, but little by little he recovered and gained weight and strength again. While he was recovering, we contacted my older sisters, Herminia and Catalina, to let them know where we were living. They came to see us as quickly as they could. Herminia was already married and brought her son, Eric to meet us for the first time. Catalina was working in the city as a housekeeper.

About two months after we were reunited with my father, Pedro, my other brother, came home. He told us that he tried to escape from the guerilla side but they caught him before he could escape.

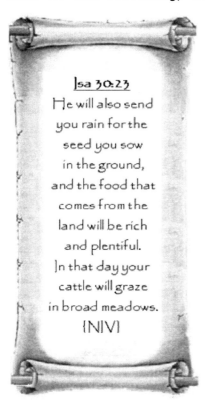

Isa 30:23

He will also send you rain for the seed you sow in the ground, and the food that comes from the land will be rich and plentiful. In that day your cattle will graze in broad meadows.

(NIV)

Victory!
The Life of José M. Mejia

They tortured him and put him in an underground prison with just one meal a day. Later he escaped and came home to us. He was sicker than my dad had been. We took him to the hospital in San Salvador where he stayed for more than a year.

When my father had recuperated from his illness, he was hired at the ranch where my uncle was working. They gave him a little piece of land to farm and God blessed every single seed that we planted there.

Chapter 6

A New Beginning

The year 1983 was a year of many challenges and life transitions for me. I was only 12 years old, yet, I was able to comprehend many things as if I were a boy of 18 years or older. Due to the fast maturity of my mind, I developed a state of confusion. Many times, when I saw children playing with toys or doing other games I felt the desire to play with them, but my mind just turned on a switch to let me know that I had more important responsibilities than play. In addition to my responsibilities, the worry of being recruited by the army or the guerrillas made the situation even worse. At this very young age, I used to offer to sell myself to work as hard as I could in the corn fields or rice fields just to earn a few pounds of rice or corn for us to eat. When my offer to work was denied, I would just pick up leftover corn cobs or rice ears, if the field owner would let me do it.

Victory!
The Life of José M. Mejía

Starting School

This picture of me was taken on January 27, 1983 when I began to attend school for the first time in my life. The picture was for my first school ID. You don't need to observe my picture very closely to see that even my smile was gone. It shows the heaviness of the giant responsibility that I was carrying. The school was about a mile from the ranch where we lived. Even though I was already 12 years old, I was only enrolled in the first grade. Because of my prior illnesses, the other students were all much bigger than I was. My first weeks in school were very hard because all the students laughed at the way I was dressed. All of them wore uniforms, but we didn't have any money for uniforms. I was dressed in an old pair of pants with a lot of patches. My shirt was in the same condition. For shoes, I wore an old pair of rubber boots.

My other problem in school was the way I spoke. Without knowing it, I was using phrases or words that were used only by the army or guerillas. The way I was speaking could have put me and my family in great danger because the conflict was still at its peak. One of the teachers let my mother know the situation, so she and my father helped me avoid those phrases and words that were not helpful to us.

To make a little money, I used to collect things to sell, like firewood and glass bottles. I also helped people at the swap meets carry their stuff. I was able to earn enough money to buy my school books, an old used uniform, and even some shoes. I wore that one old uniform to school everyday. I used to patch my shoes until the original leather was completely gone. To shine my shoes, I used soot. My breakfast was mangos that I found on the way to school and most of the time my lunch was the same delicate fruit.

My good friends and neighbors were three dogs that I kept. Many times they ate better then I did because they ate dead animals or anything they found. Sometimes I felt tempted to eat the dogs' food with them, but it was just too horrible.

Even through all this suffering and starvation, for some reason, I felt that a natural force was watching over me. I did not envy those who had everything. I was happy just to see a new day. When I look back now, I bless my God because I never knew that I was living in extreme poverty.

I learned to read and write in less than two months. Instead of my first grade diploma, they gave me my second grade diploma. I didn't care that all the students were laughing about me. The most important thing was that I had my family together again and with a decent uniform or not, I was happy enough just to be going to school.

Chapter 7
Life on the Ranch

I fully enjoyed the ranch where we were living. There were not too many people living there. Many of the people working on the ranch came from other places. Surrounding the ranch were over 3,000 acres of wild forest with a lot of animals to hunt and a lot of wild fruit. I used to climb giant trees that grew in the tropical forest. Those adventures were awesome. My joy was to bring wild fruit to my family because for me just seeing my family together was a huge dream come true. During my adventures into the forest, I would also find baby birds and bunnies and bring them home to raise and release or sometimes to sell.

There was a dairy stable on the ranch. Almost every day I would walk about a mile and a quarter to the stable to work to get a bottle of milk to feed my rabbits and wild animals. They began milking very early, so I had to start walking maybe around 2:00 a.m. or so.

Belly Up

One day, the manager of the stable challenged me to capture an old donkey that hung around the ranch. He told me if I could catch it, then it would be mine. He said the donkey was maybe 80 years old. They used to use this donkey, before the ranch had trucks, to haul milk to market. For two days I followed the donkey, but he never let me catch him. I finally caught him by making a trap in the fence with a rope. When I walked back to the stable with that donkey, the men could not believe that I really caught him. It was so old it had no teeth. They gave me a very old, dried out saddle. They helped me put it on the donkey, even though they knew it was wild. I jumped on and started riding it for about a hundred feet when the donkey popped me off. They really laughed at me, almost until they were crying. When I brought the donkey home, well actually, I had to mostly drag the donkey home, my father didn't agree with the idea of keeping it. But I begged him and told him how long it took me to catch it. My mom was there and she stepped in, telling my dad that I could keep the donkey and that made me very happy. About two months later, the donkey was getting a little tamer from working with him. I used him to carry things for me like firewood and water. He really helped me a lot.

The donkey didn't like the rain. While he had been in the wild, he would run to the stables for cover and warmth whenever it rained. Because I did not have anywhere to put him, I would keep him tied to things near our house with a rope, but there was no cover for him. One day it started raining and continued for about two weeks. I would go out and check on him every three hours to make sure he was okay. My mom would always ask me if I'd checked on him. One day when I went to see him, he was standing up and he looked serious. I went back home and my mother asked if I went to see the donkey. I told her I did. When I went back two hours later he was laying down, like he was resting. I didn't go too close, not wanting to wake him and just went back home. Later, I went back again and he was belly up! Maybe he died from the cold from such a long rain or maybe he was just old. I ran to him and he was stiff. I cried and cried. I was afraid to tell my dad because he did not want me to keep him in the first place. I went back home, shaking and crying. My sister ran to me and asked if the donkey had kicked me. I just kept crying and couldn't speak. Finally, I said, "The donkey died!" When my dad heard that he got up and said, "I told you! Now you're gonna have to pay for the donkey." He was teasing, but I thought he was serious. My sister started crying, too. And my mother and their friends just laughed at us. I finally calmed down and we went to the stable to tell the manager that the donkey was dead. He said, "Well, you owe me 100 colones." Now, I really worried because I thought he was serious, too. He said, "So, I'm gonna keep you working in the stables now." Again, I began to cry. Finally, he told me he was just joking and we went back home. My dad helped me to bury the donkey and that was the end of my transportation.

Forest Adventures

One of the many things the forest provided for us was honey, which we used in place of sugar. I would face the wild bees, taking honey from their hives for my family. Even though I didn't have any experience with honey bees and got stung once in awhile, they never really hurt me. On one occasion, I went into the forest looking for honey and came upon a dead, rotten tree with many bees flying around it. I knew there must be honey in the tree. I used the smoke from burning dried cow manure to chase away and confuse the bees, so I could get the honey. I used my machete to cut into the tree and was amazed at what I found. There was so much honey there that I had to go back home to bring my sisters to help me carry it all. There must have been five gallons or more of honey!

On another day, I went out hunting and found myself wandering farther and farther from home. I had planned to be out only for a short time and did not bring any provisions with me, such as water. It was very, very hot and I was thirsty. I was walking in the forest to the creek for water, but it was dry. I was so thirsty, but could not find any water. It was all I could think about, my thirst was so strong. My mouth was dry and my stomach was tight and cramping. I walked and walked thinking only of my thirst, until I found a small puddle. The water was dark, filled with dead, rotting leaves, animal manure, and mosquito larvae dancing all around. It was so bad, but I was so thirsty. I kneeled down and smelled the water. It was putrid and I just could not drink it. I decided to walk on to look for better water. The more I walked, the more I thought about that puddle, making me even thirstier. It was all I could think about. Finally, I turned around and went back to that puddle. Taking off my T-shirt, I placed it over the surface of the water and used it as a filter to drink the water. It smelled and tasted so bad, but after getting a small amount of it into my stomach I felt better, the cramping subsided and I was able to continue my journey back home. It is amazing to think of the longing your mind can create when you see something you want so much.

We lived on the ranch for about four years, and in that time, we created an orchard around the house from plants I found in the wild, like banana, papaya and many others. Some of the trees in the orchard were wild but most of them were fruit trees that we had planted. Many people used to tell us that there was no reason to plant too many fruit trees on land that we did not own because they said there are some fruit trees that will take five to ten years to bear fruit. My father's answer was always, "If we do not eat their fruits, someone else will eat their fruits." That was a true prophesy, because when we moved out of the ranch, somebody else moved in and ate from the trees that we had planted. God had also blessed us with many other provisions on that ranch such as corn, beans, chickens and much more.

I mentioned that three words of John 14:6 (**way, truth and life**) were taking place in my life one by one. Now the word **truth** was taking place. It was a **true** reality that my family was together, except for those that had died. The **truth** of God was

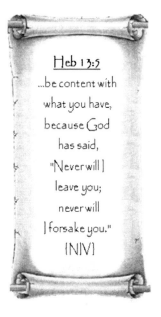

Heb 13:5

...be content with
what you have,
because God
has said,
"Never will I
leave you;
never will
I forsake you."

(NIV)

being raised in my life. It was preparing my heart to know that God had never forsaken me or my family. For some reason that I did not understand at that time, God was telling me, "I love you, my son. I have chosen you. I will be with you forever. Confide in me and you will see my Glory." Now I can see all these **truths** so clearly trough my spiritual and physical life.

Chapter *8*

A Home of Our Own

In 1985, I was fourteen years old. A new president took power in my country. By this time, our living situation had changed greatly. We had food, we had family, we had work. Life had meaning again and we had vision of a future. The president took land from the rich people, parceled it and sold it to the poor people at a very low cost. We qualified to receive a piece of land. They gave us four acres. In October of 1986, we finished building a shelter house on our new property. For the first time in our lives, we were going to live in a place that we could call **our** property. When we moved in to the new place, my father lost his job at the ranch because it was too far from our home. My sisters and I started going to our new school.

The new place had its pros and cons. The pros were that we could do anything we wanted to with the land, the town was close, and the school was better. It was more accessible to the hospital or to take the bus into the city. One problem was a shortage of water. We had to walk a mile to bring water home. We could not even dream of the possibility of having running water or electricity in our home. Also, we depended on firewood, which was scarce. We had to walk five miles or more and carry the firewood on our backs, just like we carried the water. This caused a lot of depression and fatigue for us. We were used to hard work, but this was triple hard work. To take a shower or do laundry meant we had to walk even more. There were no incomes in our family. The hard winters caused us to lose our crops. Sometimes in just one storm, we would lose everything we had planted. Everything had a beginning, but no end. We were going back to the same economic state we had been in five years before and in some ways worse. Farming was a trade that had no future. In order to improve my family's economic state, it would be necessary for me to learn another trade.

A New Direction

In 1989, at the age of nineteen, I was enrolled in a masonry school in San Salvador. Because I had not yet finished high school, I attended high school classes at night. San Salvador was about forty miles from my home. While I was going to school, I stayed with my parents friends. I would help them out with chores to pay for letting me stay there. After three months of training, I found a construction job. At this job, I earned fifteen colones for a ten-hour day. At that time, fifteen colones was worth about three American dollars. With this money, I was able to offer to pay some rent, buy food, and help my family a little bit.

Even though it was almost eight years since we had left the red zone, I had fear of and hatred for the army forces and police departments. Being in the city was torture for me, because I had to see soldiers every day. Most of the time when I saw a soldier, my body involuntarily began shaking. The color would drain from my face from the panic I felt around these people. For my sisters, it was even worse. When they saw a soldier, they would begin to cry and grab mother or whoever was with them. Sometimes they would run and try to hide themselves, the memories of past tortures still fresh in their minds. We did not have peace, because everyday we had to see soldiers or police.

The Calling

I felt I was at an age that I could avenge the abuses the army forces had done to my family. This would mean I would have to join the guerillas. One night while I was lying down (I did not say I was in bed, because I did not have one) deciding how and when to meet the guerillas to be integrated with them, something happened. I had a little radio and was listening to some music. I tuned the radio to find a better radio station. I found one with someone talking about God. As I said at the beginning of this autobiography-testimony, God protected us without our knowing Him. I had no idea God existed. This was the first time I had ever heard anything like this. We never went to church or read the Bible. I stopped to listen to that person on the radio. He was saying that God is love. When I heard the word love, immediately my mind was switched to my past and I saw all the scenes of my life and those of my family and thought, "Why is this man saying that God is love?" But for some reason I kept listening anyway. At the end of his sermon, he said, "There is a boy who is listening to us. He and his family have been through a lot of trouble. He is deciding a thing that could cost him his life." He kept saying, "Son, I know that you are listening to me. God loves you and has better plans for your life and your family. Open the door of your heart and receive Jesus as your Savior." He said, "Lift your hands in a sign of surrendering. You know what surrendering means." The word surrender was very familiar to me because it was a word used by the guerillas or army soldiers when they caught someone that was fighting against them. Surrender is a warning word, giving you just two choices, to die or to live.

My choice that night was to live. I stood and lifted my hands. When I lifted my hands up, my legs began to tremble. My hands and whole body were shaking. Something hot began to run from the tip of my fingers to the soles of my feet and I was crying. I felt my heart melting down. My tears were running incessantly over my cheeks.

The man continued, "I want to pray for you." The man prayed to Jesus for my forgiveness and made me repeat the Prayer of Faith. At the end he said, "Follow Jesus, son. Follow Jesus," and the program ended.

The next day, I thought that I had had a dream, but the desire to go back to the red zone and join the guerillas was gone. I began to see the people around me a little differently. Thoughts of God and Jesus kept shaking in my head. I went back to work, but was afraid to say what had happened to me. The day went by, the week and the whole month. My routine was the same or even worse.

More War

In November 1989, the guerillas attacked the entire country at once. The whole country was under fire. There were airplanes and helicopters bombing everywhere. Ambulances were going from one place to another. The attack lasted for thirty days. There was no work anywhere. People were dying everywhere.

In San Salvador, where I was living, hundreds of houses were destroyed. After the fighting was over, around the first week of December, I went back to work. Everything we had built was destroyed. There were legs, arms and other body parts all over the place. Many people, who had no chance of being evacuated, died in their homes. I could not stand being in a place like that any longer and went home to my parents.

Close to our village was a town that on December 17th was celebrating an annual fair and carnival with lots of music and dancing. Maybe you ask yourself, "How can these people celebrate fairs in the middle of disaster, fighting, and death?" Let me tell you that I admire my people and our courage that helps us to survive any situation. Many times the people would just hide themselves. When the battles were over, they would go out to see how many people had been killed. They would find a place to bury them and just go on as if nothing had happened. It was the only way to survive the horrors we were living with.

The Still, Small Voice

So I went to the fair with my cousins and friends. We had to walk in groups because it was too dangerous to go alone. When we got to the town, I met some of my friends that I had gone to school with. I invited one of them, Martha, to go to the carnival with me and she accepted my invitation. I paid for the tickets and gave one to her when we got to the gate. I gave my ticket to the person who was checking at the entrance.

At that moment, I heard a voice that said, "José, what are you doing in here?"

I immediately turned my head to Martha and asked, "What did you say?"

Martha replied, "I didn't say anything."

That caused worry in my heart. About an hour later, I heard the same voice, "What are you doing in here?"

I asked my friend if we could leave the carnival.

She asked, "Why? We just got here. Let's stay a little longer."

I agreed. Then for the third time I heard the voice. I once again asked my friend, "Please, let's go."

She said, "I don't want to go."

I said, "Yes, but I do want to leave this place."

Then she said, "There are my other friends. If you want to go, I will stay with them."

I said, "Okay," and left the carnival.

I found my cousins at the fair and asked if they wanted to go home. They said, "No. We will be staying here until morning."

Victory!
The Life of José M. Mejia

I was scared to go home by myself. We were five miles from home, but I was desperate to be there. It was about 11:00 p.m. and so dark I couldn't see my hands in front of my face. I decided to go home by myself anyway.

I began to walk with a great fear in me. After I left that town there was silence all around me. The only thing I could hear were roosters crowing and barking of dogs. As I walked, I said, "God, I promise I will never be in a place like that ever again." Tears began to run over my cheeks and a fear of God inundated my being. Most of the time, I was running, desperate to be home. I just wanted to talk with someone about what had happened, about that voice I kept hearing.

When I arrived home, my father was awake. He said, "I was worried about you. Who came with you?"

I said, "No one came with me, I walked home alone. All my cousins are going to stay at the fair until morning."

He asked me what happened. I told him that nothing happened, that I just didn't feel good and decided to come back home. I just didn't know how to tell him. I laid down for a while, many thoughts going through my head. I knew we had not been believers and I didn't know how to begin. Finally, I got up to talk with my dad.

I said to him, "I have to tell you why I left the fair. God spoke to me with an audible voice. The voice asked what I was doing at that carnival. It happened three times. That's why I left the carnival and the fair. And when I was walking home I promised God that I would never be in a place like that ever again."

My father replied, "Be obedient and listen to that voice. Maybe He has chosen you."

Decision

The next day, I went back to San Salvador, the city where I used to work. I heard people talk about the United States. They had family there who were doing pretty well because a lot of work was available. Listening to that put the idea in my head to go to the United States. I had nothing to lose except my family, but felt I might be able to help them more from the United States than by staying in El Salvador.

When I told my parents of my plans, they were shocked. They said they didn't want to lose another son. They asked me to stay and struggle with them and maybe one day things would change and we would have better opportunities. I told them, "No. We have struggled too much already, so I am going to try this adventure." Even though I didn't have enough money to take with me, I decided to start the journey anyway.

Chapter 9

The Long Journey

The scene when I left my home is as fresh in my mind today as it was then, January 17, 1990. My parents blessed me. My mother leaned against a post that was holding up our rickety house. She was crying and waving her hands. That scene broke my heart into a thousand pieces. Weeping, I left my family and my country. I had no idea where I was going. I carried with me just one extra pair of pants and a shirt. I walked to the highway and hopped on a bus to San Salvador. I had just enough money to get from San Salvador to Guatemala City by bus. From there, I was going to be at God's mercy.

I had obtained a permit to get as far as Guatemala City. To go further was illegal. When I left the city to continue toward the United States, I had to be hidden from authorities. I didn't have enough money to bribe the Guatemalan police, so I had to hide at all costs. Slipping on without being seen, I took short rides in buses or vans, making my way toward the border. After traveling for three days, I reached the Guatemala/Mexico border, crossing the river into Mexico. That was the beginning of my great suffering in Mexico.

Because I had no money, I had to walk along the highway or through pastures near the highway for days. Some days I ate once a day, many days, not at all. When I asked for help, some people denied me. Other people would provide me with food. I was beaten by some Mexican land owners for trespassing. They threatened to turn me in to the Mexican Police, but I begged them and they let me go. Sometimes I would ask for rides, other times I would jump on cargo trains, but mostly I just walked.

After three months, I reached Mexico City, where I stayed for about a week, hiding from the authorities and trying to rest and recover a bit before continuing my journey. To leave the city, I jumped another cargo train.

I recall one time when I was walking on the highway, a truck had stopped and the driver was checking the truck's tires and other things. I asked him if he could give me a ride. He asked me where I was going.

I said, "Sir, I don't want to lie to you. I am trying to reach the U.S.A."

He said, "You are crazy, Morro." Morro is a slang word that most Mexican people use to say "boy." He continued, "Do you want me to lose my job or to be caught by the Federales and be accused of being a coyote?" He was referring to people who smuggle illegal people to the U.S.A.

His response did not surprise me because my requests for help had been turned down many times during my journey. I said, "I'm sorry, but I didn't mean that, sir."

So, I just kept walking down the road. Suddenly the man called out to me. "Hey, Morro, come back." I went back to where he was parked. He said, "I will make a space on the back of the trailer for you to ride."

I wondered, "What could have made him change his mind?" Even though I was worried about it, I decided to go with him. He was hauling smashed cars and pieces of junk metal. He removed some pieces of junk to make space for me. I crawled into the pile of metal and he used those pieces to cover me. I heard the door of the truck bang and felt it move forward as we started down the road.

It seemed like we traveled for hours. My legs and most of my body were numb from sitting in one position for so long. The metal was pressing in on me. The driver didn't stop until he reached what must have been a checkpoint. I could see only out the back of the truck and not what was in front of us.

I heard voices say, "Where are you going?"

"To the metal processor," somebody answered. I supposed it was the driver.

"Are you smuggling anything illegal in that chaterrero?" someone asked him. Chaterrero is a word that means junk or piles of metal.

"No." the driver replied.

Through the holes I could see they were Mexican soldiers. I was praying to God that they would not discover me. Some soldiers were walking around the truck and poking the chaterrero with rebar and stepping on the metal. Then I heard a squealing sound going through the metal straight toward my chest. I gasped and held my breath when I saw the tip of the rebar coming at me. I could not move to avoid it, but suddenly the rebar stopped and was pulled back before it reached me. I exhaled with relief. I closed my eyes and tears started running down my face. The inspection lasted twenty minutes or more. They finally let the truck go.

About an hour later, the driver stopped again and I thought maybe there was another inspection station. But this time the driver got out of the truck and called out, "Morro, are you still there?"

"Yes!", I replied.

He climbed on the trailer and helped me get out of my hiding place. When he lowered me to the ground I just fell right down. My body was numb and my legs cramping. He helped me to stretch my legs out and said, "I can not take you any farther because I am going to take another highway that is not going to the north." He gave me some of his food and a bottle of water. I thanked him and watched as he drove off leaving me there at the crossroad in the highway.

I found a place in the bushes beside the highway to rest awhile before continuing my journey. After a night of resting, I began walking along the highway again. Sometimes I would take shortcuts through fields when I could see the highway was curving in the distance. I always tried to keep the highway in view so I wouldn't get lost. During one of these shortcuts, I met a guy who was plowing his land with the help of a pair of mules. I asked him if he could give me a job or if I could do some work for food.

He said, "Oh, yeah! I was needing a helper because I need to pile up all these rocks that I am uncovering while I'm plowing." He offered to pay me 20 pesos a day and food.

I said, "That's good enough."

So I started that day, walking after the plow, piling up the rocks. The man fed me one or two meals each day and let me stay in a little barn that he had by his house. After a week, I told him I needed my money because I wanted to continue going north. He said, "Well, I do not have any money to pay you. Maybe when I harvest the crop I can give you something." I didn't say anything to that, just looked at him. I decided to leave anyway. When I was leaving his place, he said, "Hey! If you want, here is a jacket that somebody left here the other day. If you want, you can take it." I took the jacket and left. It wasn't the money he owed me, but at least I wasn't leaving with empty hands.

I do not remember exactly the place this farm was at, but I remember some people mentioning a city called Selalla that could have been in the state of Guanajuato. I continued traveling in the same way, jumping cargo trains, getting rides in cars or vans or just walking.

Sometime later in my travels, I reached a bus station. They called it Central Comionera of Chihuahua. I was very cold and went into the station to try to get warm. I sat down, pretending I was waiting to take a bus. I was very frightened because there were Federales and police officers in the bus station, but I needed to get my body warmed. I felt someone touch my shoulder from behind me. I was scared thinking, it was a Federale. This person said, "Son, I'm catching a bus right now. Take this jacket and put it on." He placed the jacket over my shoulders and quickly moved away. I didn't have much chance to see his face because he was standing behind me. I just saw people walking toward the station where his bus must have been coming into. I thanked God that it was an old man touching me and not a Federale. I left the station with the jacket to continue my journey.

Victory!
The Life of José M. Mejía

God Provides

I don't know where I was when I reached the U.S. border, only that I was walking in a very dry and sandy land. I had walked for a week in the desert with no food and very little water. The only water I found were small puddles that were trapped in the rocks after a rain. I remember it was cloudy most days and very cold. The low temperatures caused pain in my body. I had collected a few more pieces of clothing during my journey through Mexico and wore these extra layers for warmth. At night I would try to find a place to sleep among the rocks and trees to hide from the wind and rains.

One night, I finally sat in the sand, exhausted, feeling like starvation would be my end. My eyes were blurry, my whole body shook from hunger and thirst. I had not another ounce of strength to go on. Looking to Heaven, I cried out to God, "If you are real, God, please don't let me die in this desert. I have a mother and father to support. Please, help me."

At that moment, it seemed that I fell into a deep sleep. I don't know how long I slept, but it was very dark and foggy when I finally

John 6:31

Our forefathers ate the manna in the desert; as it is written: 'He gave them bread from heaven to eat.'

(NIV)

woke and opened my eyes. I saw there by my side a white spot on the sand. Still groggy from sleep and starvation, I slowly reached out and touched it. That white spot was tortillas; cold, fresh, tortillas! I grabbed them and began eating. As I ate, my body began to warm up and I felt the energy to continue my journey. Even though I had only eaten a small amount of food, my body felt refreshed, as if I had been given a full meal. I felt like I had come from a very cold place to stand before a warm fire.

My Beloved, God knows your needs one hundred percent. He knows what is going to strengthen your body, spirit, and soul. He knows perfectly what you like to eat most. In my case, He could have provided me with any other kind of food, but He knew that my main nutritional diet was **tortillas.** I didn't ask Him about food or tell Him what kind of food I wanted. He knew what I needed.

When I asked God, "Please, do not let me die in this desert," what I meant was, "Take me to a place where I can meet people and ask them for help." But my God is everything, He knows everything and He provides what is best for us. He took me out from the **real desert.** He strengthened me. He provided all the resources to meet my needs. Then and now, He is continuously providing and supplying for all my needs. I don't know what kind of desert you are walking in at this very moment or maybe you have thoughts that God, the Almighty One, has forsaken you. Let me tell you that He is there with you wherever you are. He is watching over you and He will take care of you and will take you to green pastures where the springs of fresh water will flow to refresh your dry land, your desert (Psalms 23). God is awesome. He is real. His word is truly powerful and full of life and real promises. At this very moment, my heart is full of joy to know that we have a great God in Heaven.

Again the faithfulness of God's word took place in my life. He showed me the way out of the desert. He gave me life again and showed me His mercy.

Chapter 10

In the Land of My Dreams

I continued to walk once again until I reached a city whose name I don't know to this day. I did know I was in the United States because most of the people spoke English.

Somehow, I was able to make contact with some of my relatives that had left the country before the war. They wired me some money and I was able to take a bus to Pasadena, California, where they resided. It was almost impossible to believe I was in the United States in North America, where I thought my troubles were over. But that was not true.

I was staying with these relatives who told me, "In this country, everybody is equal. We had to pay for rent, food, and bills since the first day that we came here and for you, there is no difference." I had no choice. They told me, "There is a place you can go to look for a job. That place is on the sidewalk at Villa and Fair Oak."

The first barrier I faced was the language barrier. I did not know any English. The first man I met on that street corner was also looking to find work. Thankfully, he spoke Spanish as did many others there. He invited me to go to church with him. My heart was desperate to see what churches looked like. Even though God saved me back in El Salvador, I had never been to a church. I went with him and in that church, God touched me again. I kept going to church whenever it was possible.

I wrote to let my parents know for the first time in six months where I was and that news filled their hearts with joy.

Over two weeks went by and every day I was on that street corner, yet I didn't work a single day. After two weeks, a man picked me up and took me to break concrete and dig trenches for one whole week. I was so grateful to be working. One day he said, "I'll pick you up tomorrow." That was Saturday and he never came back again. I had worked for a whole week and he didn't pay me a single cent.

Many times things like that happened, however others were good to me. Going to church, I met many friends, some like me or even worse. We prayed to God that with the little money I was making, I could pay my bills and help my parents. Another good thing that happened was that I was able to reunite with my sister, Herminia who had come to the United States sometime earlier than me. It was good to know some family was near me.

About six months after I arrived here, I began to go to school with my friend to learn English. I didn't have a clue what the teacher was saying in the class or what he was teaching. I think the white board knew more than I did, because all the writing was on it.

One night on our way to school, we were in a car accident. I had three cuts on my face. This accident sent me to the hospital for a week. The hospital bill came to over $8,000. Before I was completely healed, I had to go back to the street to look for a job to pay this bill, as well as all my other living expenses. As time passed, I continued going to the street to find odd jobs here and there and attending school and church. This was the way of my life for the next three years.

Remember I spoke about those three words from God taking place in my life; way, truth, and life? You see that God was directing my **way** in this new country, but the **way** was always through His Son, Jesus. The friend He sent who took me to church that first time, solidified the **way** God would have me go, always keeping me connected to the Body of Christ.

Working

In 1994, a man picked me up with three other men. He was a plumber. We went to help him dig a very deep trench for a sewer line. After we finished the job, he paid us and asked for our phone numbers. A week later, he called me and took me to work again. By this time, I was speaking a little English, as well as understanding it.

God used the plumber. God laid the path before this man so he would keep me working with him and teach me his skill. One day Dan surprised me with a box full of the basic tools used in plumbing. He told me, "José, I want you to learn what I know. I will teach you as much as I can about plumbing." And he did it.

Never in my life had I driven a car. Dan also taught me to drive a car. God blessed his business and provided a lot of work for us. I had applied for a work permit. They gave me that permit under political asylum. With the permit, I was able to have a driver's license and a social security number. To have steady work was a blessing as it allowed me to send some money back home to help my family. I was keeping in touch with my family through letters and phone calls. We had contact a couple of times a month.

One Ending, Another Beginning

In 1998, I received a call from my sister, Jilma, in El Salvador. She told me, "José, our mother has died." She had committed suicide. That news made me crazy. Never in any of our conversations had she expressed a desire to die. I asked my dad and sisters what they knew about her state of mind. No one expressed any idea that she was so depressed. I could only imagine that all the tortures of her life during the invasions caused her to do such a thing. Or perhaps because all of her children were living away from her, her mind made her feel she had lost us all in the upheaval. I am only guessing, because she left us no clues. I did not know what to do. I went to the immigration department to see if they could give me a permit to go to my mother's funeral, but they denied it. The only thing that I could do was swallow all that pain and be more attached to God. I gave thanks to God even for my mother's death. God filled my heart with His peace. Even though I did not understand it, I trusted in God's plan.

In the same year as my mother's death, I met Bob Williams. Once in a while he used to do tractor work for my boss. The first day I met him we were in the city of Arcadia, California. He told me that he had a ranch. He used most of his property to board horses and asked me if I would be interested in helping him take care of the place. I wasn't sure about it but a week later, I went to see the ranch. I liked it because it was out of the city, so I decided to move to Bob's ranch. He offered me $50 a week and an old trailer to live in. Somehow, I accepted the offer because that would save a little money on rent. To clean that place and feed the horses used to take about two and a half or three hours every day. I had to get up at 4:30 in the morning to clean the corral and feed the horses because I had to be at my plumbing job at 7:30 a.m. Besides that I was going to school and attending church regularly. One man who rented a trailer at the ranch used to get up and yell at me because I was making noise when I raked the corral. I lasted there for a year and then moved out because it was too much for me. Bob and I had become friends and even though I left his ranch I remained in touch with him from time to time.

Dan's business had grown so much that he partnered with another plumber and incorporated it. He had already bought me a truck and I had all my tools on it. The truck was my personal transportation, also. About six months after my boss partnered with the other plumber, he was hit by a car, which broke his skull, ribs, and a leg. This accident left Dan in a coma for a year and disabled him for the rest of his life. I missed working with him very much. He had taught me so many skills over the years and treated me like a friend. It was almost like he had died in that accident.

I was never really able to develop a good working relationship with the new owner. The work environment was difficult for me and grew worse over time. I kept working for the company for another year. Things changed so much in the company that I just left the truck and tools and went back to the street corner where my boss had picked me up five years earlier. I had a lot of friends there and when I was working for Dan, the plumber, we used to hire them to work for us. When they saw me walking down the sidewalk, they thought I was going to pick them up for work. I told them, "No, I've come to be a partner with you. I do not have a job now." We all just laughed.

The Test

I had been going to the street for about two days. There were about twenty men around me. I was sharing the gospel of Jesus Christ with them and telling them stories when a white van with blue stripes went by. I lifted my head and saw the driver make a signal for me to cross the street. Nobody else saw that, so I said goodbye to my friends and crossed the street. About five minutes later, the van came back to pick me up.

The man barely asked my name. I asked him, "What do you do?"

When he heard that I spoke English he was surprised and said, "So, you speak English."

Victory!
The Life of José M. Mejía

I said, "Not very well, but I think that I do enough to understand you."

He said, "I am a plumber."

I replied, "Oh, really? I am a plumber, too."

He said, "You are lying. Why would a plumber be on the street like you were?" He continued, "Many people say that they know something just to get a job, but in reality they know nothing."

I said, "I am not lying, sir. I bet I know many things that you know."

He replied, "I will test you today."

When we got to the job, he told me, "I am remodeling this bathroom. In my van are all the materials. Go get them. Get all the tools you think you need because I am going to leave you here. I have another job."

I said, "Okay," and went to grab all that was necessary. I told him, "I am ready, sir, now you can leave."

He just explained where he wanted the shower valve and drains, then left me to do the work. I worked hard that day by myself to finish the job the way my new boss wanted it. When he came back at around 5:00 p.m., I had everything done. He just smiled and said, "You are hired."

He paid me pretty well that day. He said, "I do a lot of plumbing work around Los Angeles county and bordering cities. I will keep you with me for at least three months until you learn how to read maps and how to find addresses as quickly as possible, because I have a lot of emergency jobs." He didn't keep his promise of training me to read maps for three months. After just two weeks, he was sending me to do jobs by myself. For me, it was okay because he found out I was able to get around without him. God blessed his business so much that it was hard for us to get to all the calls. Even though I was tired of driving in that heavy LA traffic, I was making pretty good money and that kept me going. I was able to send some home and even save some.

More Trouble

In May of 2000, my father called me and said, "Son, I am having problems here. I have already found two notes on my patio without names on them, asking me for a great amount of money. The note says that if I don't take that money to the place they had written down on the specified day they are going to kill me or kidnap one of my daughters and that if I let the police know, the threat will be worse."

I told him, "Don't be afraid, Dad. Go and inform the police department."

The police didn't do anything. They said they can't do anything with a simple piece of paper. A month later the kidnappers came to his home wearing masks. They broke the doors open, stole and destroyed as much as possible. They told my dad they were not joking. They did not harm my dad, but threatened him badly, telling him that they wanted the money, so all my savings went to pay those guys. It was worth all the money I had to feel the relief of knowing my dad was once again safe from harm.

Chapter 11

Answered Prayers

At the beginning of 2002, now 31 years old, I made contact with Bob Williams again. He told me, "José, I bought a new property in northern California. It is a pretty place in the countryside. It is very quiet with a lot of wildlife. I would like you to come and try your luck over there with us."

I told him I would like to try it, but asked how the work was in that area. He said, "That is a problem because there are not very many people in that area, but you can stay at my house as long as you want."

I prayed God would help me decide what to do. Was it His will for me to move to a different place that I didn't know? But God gave a positive answer in my heart to move on. I asked God for three things if I moved to a new place. I asked Him to provide me a church where I could praise Him freely, a job, and a place to live.

The first day at the Williams' house, I liked it. This place is so pretty. It's in the country near Coarsegold, California, about 22 miles south of Yosemite National Park. But when I walked around the property, I just saw oak trees and wild grass. My heart doubted for a moment. I asked God, "How am I going to make a living in this place?"

God spoke to my heart and said, "Trust in me and I will provide everything for you." True to His word, God provided a good job and I still live at Bob Williams' as of this writing.

The first month here, I helped Bob fix a lot of things around his place. Later a neighbor hired me to help him clean up his place. Over time I was hired to do many odd jobs for people living in the area. Soon I found full-time work for a carpenter as a handyman. When it appeared that I would be staying, Bob brought in a trailer to the property, so I could set up a home for myself.

God Sends More Angels

About a month after arriving at Bob's, I met Don Cardoza, a friend of Bob's, who was a member of a local church. One Sunday, he took me to his church, Yosemite Lakes Community Church, and I felt that it was my church, too. The music was anointing and the sermon, too. The problem was that my English was not fully developed to understand the whole sermon or the songs. But I didn't care much about that. I said, "With God's help I will understand this language fully." I said to God, "God, I don't know what those musicians are playing or singing, but one day I would like to be a part of that music group." I didn't know much about music, but knew that God was going to give me that opportunity.

One morning I met Jim Trimble, who was the bass player for the church band. He adopted me into his family immediately. At the end of the service, he invited me to go to his house. I met his family, who are all wonderful people. I told him that I was interested in learning some music.

He said, "Oh, yes. I will teach you." The next Monday night I went with him to a practice at the church and kept going with him to every practice for about three months. There was a pair of congas at the church that no one used. The director of the group asked if I knew how to play congas.

I said, "No, I don't know how to play congas, but I can learn." So I began to practice and I bought a book of conga lessons.

Learning to play congas gave me the opportunity to stay in the group. But the instrument I really wanted to learn was the bass guitar, so I kept one ear open for the congas and the other for the bass guitar. Once in awhile, I stopped playing congas to watch Jim and asked him questions about the bass rhythms. Sometimes at practices, Jim would help me play the bass. A year later, they gave me an opportunity to play bass guitar at the general service. From then on, when Jim would go to Mexico or somewhere else, I would play bass guitar in the church band for him.

In April of 2004, Dr. Cody Gunderson, the Senior Pastor of the church, gave me the opportunity to share some of my testimony at church. God touched many people in that service. That same month, he recommended me to go with a team from the church to the rescue mission in Madera, California. Since then, I have gone to the rescue mission for over three years. It has been a blessing because we are able to reach not only those people who speak English, but also those who speak Spanish. Being part of the rescue mission team has been a school of training for me. God has developed in me the ability to be a translator from English to Spanish or from Spanish to English. Most of the time, my job at the rescue mission is being an interpreter. That is a wonderful experience in my life. While this gift was not in my plans, it was in God's plan. Many times, I translated for myself as I shared the good news of salvation. God has used us for His Glory at the rescue mission. Hundreds of souls have been saved.

Back to School

Since arriving in America, my desire to continue my education had always remained strong. In my country, I barely finished the ninth grade. As I reflected on my school days in El Salvador, the longing to go back to school came into my heart again. I didn't know the area very well, so I wasn't sure what schools were available. A friend of Bob's helped me find one.

In August, 2003 I enrolled in an independent adult high school. The name of the school is Yosemite Adult High School in Oakhurst, California, just eleven miles north of Coarsegold.

My teacher's name was Roberta Savolskis. She was my teacher and came to be my best friend at the school. At the beginning, my English was so bad that I spent a whole semester just reading and writing English, which disturbed my brain neurons. By the second semester I began to take some other classes but English continued to be my daily food and continues even now, because I am still learning the English language. What a language to learn! Even now, I am using the help of a friend to edit this book so you can understand what I am trying to tell you!

Even with the struggles of learning English, I put all my effort into succeeding in all my subjects. This was not easy considering that I was working full time. I was also caretaker of Bob's place, which by the way, is like a zoo, with a wide variety of animals to care for, horses, dogs, cats, chickens, cows, and much more. We had a large garden and small orchard, not to mention all the beautiful flower beds to care for. I was also creating landscaping around my trailer, building retaining walls, and planting flowers for my enjoyment. My life was very full.

In addition to all this stuff, I was attending church every week. Twice a month I was traveling about thirty-nine miles to preach at the rescue mission in Madera. Many times, exhausted, I had to drag myself to school or to do my homework. I used to sleep only four hours a night, but I never gave up.

To earn my high school diploma, I needed a little more than two hundred credits. The task felt like a never-ending tunnel. But I had a goal in my mind and that goal was to earn my high school diploma at any cost.

Finally, by the first semester of 2006, my teacher told me that I was going to have enough credits to graduate that semester. In order to graduate, I had to present a senior project and pass the California Exit Exam. Even though it was very difficult, I passed the Exit Exam without completely melting my brain. I then began my senior project.

My Senior Project

My teacher gave me a list of topics to choose from for my senior project. It took me a month to decide. Time was running short and this put a lot pressure on me. Finally, I chose photography for my project and borrowed some cameras. I spent many days in Yosemite National Park taking pictures, walking through all the beautiful scenes of this park. Sometimes, I would carry two or more cameras to compare pictures of the same scene. I read many books by and about Ansel Adams, a famous photographer of the park. I took some pictures that could have been the same scenery that Ansel Adams photographed. A month later, my senior project began to take form. It was going to be presented on May 17, 2006. By May 5, my project was completed with a lot of work and enormous help from Joan Cardoza.

The day of my senior project presentation finally arrived. I was very nervous because I was going to be speaking in front of seven or more judges. They were going to judge my speech and the quality of my project. My heart was pounding fast and hard. This was the first speech of my life and it was going to be judged. My English was still a barrier to me and that increased my nervousness.

The moment came. My teacher stood up and introduced me to the judges, giving them a brief speech about me. Then she said, "The stage is yours, José."

I said, "Thanks," and calmly started spreading my work out on the table. My breathing showed I was a little nervous. I asked for an easel, which was provided by my teacher. Then I greeted the judges. I really emphasized all of my teacher's wonderful support. I thanked the school board and other teachers who had helped me. Some of the judges had big smiles, while others barely smiled. And some of them did not smile at all, but that didn't bother me, because I was determined to do the very best presentation that I could. All of the judges were silent. I started my speech by explaining why I had chosen to do my project on photography and, little by little, I brought them to my project journal. I described my photographs with careful detail, such as what camera I had used and what each photo meant to me. The room was in complete silence. I felt that I was speaking just to the four walls of the classroom. I showed them what kind of cameras Ansel Adams had used and how he had developed his pictures. Because of the utter silence, my nerves wanted to open the door of the classroom and run away. After 15 minutes or so, I concluded my presentation, giving thanks to the judges for the opportunity to present my project to them. I opened time for the judges to ask me questions, which many of them did. I was so well-prepared that without a doubt, I gave them all satisfactory answers. Finally, my presentation was complete. That was a big relief to me. The judges stood up and, with smiles, they all applauded me.

The next day I went to class. Ms. Salvolskis was so happy. The first thing she said to me was, "You know what, José? The judges gave you the highest score! They were so impressed with your project. You have no idea how they were talking about your project. And besides that, they chose you to be one of the three students to speak at the graduation ceremony."

The last part of her news made the nervousness that I had thrown away just one day before come back. She continued, "I know that you will do a good job, the only thing is that on graduation day, there will be over three hundred people in attendance."

When I heard that, I felt like something was pulling my ears up and down, but I accepted the challenge. The first thing God put in my mind was to begin the speech with the scripture that is in Philippians, Chapter 4, Verse 13, **"I can do all things through Christ which strengtheneth me."** {KJV}(Emphasis added)

Later that week, I presented a rough draft of my speech to my teacher. She said, "It looks pretty good. Just do it as naturally as you can."

Graduation At Last!

The graduation ceremony was held on June 9, 2006. The graduates arrived at the auditorium an hour early. Their family and friends began to arrive and in less than 30 minutes, there were over two hundred people in the auditorium, including many of my friends. Most of the students were already sitting down. The ceremony began with introductions of the staff members and people who support the school. After these presentations, the first student chosen to speak was called. I felt an overwhelming urge to take off that black robe and hat I was wearing and run away. Luckily, it was not me they had called. The student who spoke had written down her entire speech. It sounded really good. That made me even more nervous. The audience on one side shouted louder than the other side. Then the

Victory!
The Life of José M. Mejia

next student to speak was called. Even though both these students were speaking in their native language, they had written down their speeches to read and I didn't understand the reason for that.

When I heard their speeches, my mind was mixed with anxiety and many other emotions that I can't describe. Finally, the person who was directing the ceremony said, "To continue our program, I would like to present our last speaker who is graduating from Yosemite Adult High School, José M. Mejia." Some of my friends stood up and shouted. I felt like someone took my heart away. I think that my color went from brown to yellow, but I just took a deep breath and walked up to the platform.

Someone handed me a microphone. To one side of me were about 50 members of the staff and in front of me, over three hundred people. I wished that something would happen to that microphone, so that nobody could hear me, but instead the microphone was so loud that even the last spider in the farthest corner of that auditorium was able to hear me.

I had not written down my speech. Not because I was lazy, but because I had just decided to do it that way, to let my heart flow freely. There were hundreds of eyes watching me. A minute after I had started my speech everything was completely silent— again! I felt like I was the king of the auditorium. All my nervousness was gone. I had a few notes with me, but I forgot to use them. My speech was short. I don't think it was over seven minutes long. I concluded my speech by thanking the staff members and the audience and hung up the microphone. The silence continued for another few seconds and then the staff members began to stand up, applauding, followed by the whole audience. Many people were saying "Bravo! Bravo!" I could not believe what I was hearing!

Grinning in amazement, I went back to my seat and the first student was called to receive his diploma. After all the diplomas were presented, they called the honor students. They called them by their achievement, by the school they attended, and then by their names. I felt relief that the ceremony would soon be over and my part had been completed successfully.

When the last of the honor students received their recognition, the program announcer began to say, "In recognition of academic achievement, good citizenship, and outstanding community service, we, the Madera County School Board Association, commend your exceptional qualities that contribute to our effort in building bright futures and strong communities in Madera County. It is my honor to present this certificate of honor to **José M. Mejia.**"

I was stunned to hear my name! It touched my heart deeply. As if in one voice, I heard the whole audience saying, "Yeah!" So I walked again to the platform to receive my certificate of achievement. Cameras were flashing from all directions. I hugged my teacher and shook hands with many others before returning to my seat. The smile on my face showed the joy I felt in my heart.

Then my teacher took the microphone and said, "The teachers and staff of Yosemite Adult High School, for his academic excellence, unanimously honor a student that with great effort has proven that nationality is not a barrier for achievement. And for us it is a pleasure to give this honor to **José M. Mejia**!" Again, the screaming rose up. That was awesome! I gave all those ovations to God, the Creator of Heaven and Earth! Hallelujah! To Jesus the

Victory!
The Life of José M. Mejia

Savior of my soul. Because of all this wonderful encouragement and the two scholarships I had been awarded, I went on to begin my college education.

Chapter 12

My Father is Saved

In the first week of August, 2007, I received a call from my brother, Arturo, in El Salvador. The call was to let me know that my father was dying. Even at seventy years old, he continued farming a little piece of land that he had. While working on his farm, he was spraying a chemical weed killer. The chemical was so strong he absorbed it through his skin. The skin covering his body was severely damaged by the chemical. The chemical reached his lungs, liver, pancreas, kidneys, and intestines. He was bleeding internally. The sides of his body under his ribs were decaying and full of infection. The doctors gave him a 1% chance of survival.

We put him in a private hospital, which cost a lot of money. I had saved a little money and was trying to buy a house. Instead, I used it to pay for my father's hospital bills. I prayed to God about his healing. The rescue mission team and many other people from the church prayed for him. A week later, after he arrived at the hospital, I received an emergency call from my sister Catalina who was in El Salvador. She said, "I think that our father died. It's been over twenty minutes and he's not responding to any C.P.R." I just sat down to pray and ask God for mercy on my dad.

After twenty minutes he came back to life. Three weeks later, because of the doctor's knowledge and God's mercy, he began to respond to the medications. He began to eat and to speak. God had healed him. God had answered our prayers! God had performed a miracle in my father's life! Glory be to the Almighty One and to Jesus, our Savior, Creator of the Heaven and Earth!

My dad stayed in the hospital for a little more than two months. The doctors grafted skin to cover the areas of his body that were damaged. A week after they did the skin graft, they sent him home with no medication. All the doctors told him that he would not need any more medicine.

A month later, I asked him what happened when he was not responding to the C.P.R. He said, "Son, I do not remember about that, but one thing I do remember is that I went to a horrible place that I wouldn't wish anyone would have to go to." He described the place that he went to like this, "I began to go to a dark hole. At the beginning of the hole were sparkles coming to me. As I was going deeper in the hole, there were no more sparkles. The sparks were turned into flames. The flames were growing as I was going deeper into that hole. Still deeper, I began to hear people screaming, asking for help in desperate voices. I began to scream, too, because the smell and the heat of those flames were horrible. There was not a way out, just a way in. As I was going deeper, the torment was greater and more horrifying. I do not understand how I got out from there," he said, "but when I woke up, there were a lot of doctors, nurses, and my daughters around me crying."

Let me tell you, this chilled my skin. I told him, "What you described is what the Bible calls hell. You went to hell, Dad!" I exclaimed again, "What you described is what the Bible calls hell! You went to hell, Dad!"

My father does not know how to read, so he had never read the Bible. Nor had he ever gone to church. "Dad, have you ever received Jesus in your heart as your Savior?" I asked him.

He said, "Son, one time I did it, but not with my heart. I did it just to avoid all the people coming to bother me with that Jesus name, or religion. I did not even pray myself. I just let them do all the talking."

I explained the plan of salvation to him and asked him if he would like to receive Jesus as his Savior now.

Dad understood that meant he would spend eternity in Heaven with Jesus. He said, "Yes, son. I want to receive Jesus with my heart now."

"Yes, Jesus!" I exclaimed.

I guided him in the repentance prayer. My father confessed his sins and received Jesus as his Savior with his own lips and in his own heart! That was another victory to glorify Jesus Christ, our Savior! Hallelujah! Glory to God in Heaven and peace to men!

Let me tell you, the devil is not happy and I don't care if he is happy or not! The only thing I care about is pleasing God. One more time God has proven His mercy, His love, and His great power to us.

Chapter 13

Looking Back

How painful it has been for me to write this journal, as I mentally walked through the places where deep wounds were cut in my physical and moral life, as well as in my family's and in many other innocent lives.

Even though my childhood was surrounded by pain and suffering, my family and I never devoted our lives to the crushing of the difficulties that we had to face every day. We always found a reason to live and to be thankful for being alive. In those moments when bullets were not flying over our heads, we used any resource that was available to enjoy each minute of our lives. We never thought of the suffering and poverty as an ending road. We lived day by day just hoping to see the coming night. Seeing a new day and a new night was a daily victory.

The tears of my mother, the screaming of my sisters, the buzz of the bullets, the concussions of the bombs, the loud noise of the jets and helicopters in some ways are still fresh in my memory, but now by the Grace of Jesus Christ, I am overcoming all those tragedies.

Fleeing every day, gathering firewood, eating dry, uncooked meat, edible plants, and fruit were not just a challenge but a great risk. Just picking a mango to mitigate my starvation could cost my life, because I never knew when an underground bomb would explode and blow my body into only a hundred pieces, if I was lucky. Going in and out of the conflict zone at my age was not to prove my bravery. It was the enormous need that we had that forced me to risk my short life every day at any cost.

Leaving my parents living in extreme poverty and departing to an unknown country was not a luxury. Leaving them in the condition that they were in was the most painful decision I would ever make. Especially, seeing again the flow of tears from my mother's eyes was like mutilating my body.

James 1:2-3

Consider it pure joy, my brothers, whenever you face trials of many kinds, because you know that the testing of your faith develops perseverance.

[NIV]

Each time that I had to hop on a cargo train brought the possibility of facing death. Starvation and cold were not on another planet. They were at my side just waiting to achieve their goal. Being in a place that only God could see was never in my plans. Reaching the destination that I had in my mind when I left my country was not to tell the world of my greatness. Being in the place where I am right now is not because I deserve it. All this is for the Mercy, Grace and

Victory!
The Life of José M. Mejia

Glory of the Lord.

As I am concluding this part of my journal, I ask forgiveness from all the authorities to which God had given the control to guard their countries, especially to the authorities of Guatemala, Mexico, and the United States and to all you people.

Job 19:25 says: **"I know that my Redeemer lives, and that in the end he will stand upon the earth."** {NIV}(Emphasis added) Those words talk to me all the time and I can say the same thing. I know that my redeemer lives. He has lifted me up from the dust and from the most worthless things of the world. He has never let me down. He has been my shield, my provider, my comfort, my strength, the sun that has shined over my head, and the arms that have sustained me. God has been my food and my water, my bed and my shelter, the reason for my life, the refuge from my storms, and the builder of my laugh.

One thing I always ask God in my prayers is that He never will let me forget how my family and I used to live and where we have been. No matter where I am today or why I am there is not reason enough to forget what God has done in our lives. What can I do to repay God for all His love and mercy that He has put over me and my family? There is not money enough in this world that can pay for God's faithfulness. I love You, God!

Epilogue

All that you have read in this book is real. I am so thankful to God for all the things that I have been through. Maybe nothing similar to this has happened to you. With a sincere heart I pray to God that nothing like this ever happens to you. Many times the things that happen during our lifetimes do not make sense to us, but in God's will they have a purpose.

I plead with you that if something in this testimony impacted your life, read it again. Compare my life with the life that you have had or have right now. See yourself carefully. See how rich you are. Maybe since you were born you've had your own room, your own bed, or more than one toy, plenty of care, food, and much more.

When you were cold, did you have a shelter or someone to cover you? Are you thankful for what you have had and have now? Can you identify yourself with all the things that have happen to me? If so, don't worry. God still loves you as you are.

If your past has been hard or your life now is hard, do not anchor your life to the ugly things of the past. Stop for a moment and review the journey of your life. Then compare it with the beautiful things that you have enjoyed. Bury the ugly past and anchor yourself to the beautiful things that you will enjoy from now on. There are many ways to reach our goals. Better things are waiting for you and for me in this life and in the Kingdom of God. No matter if the day is cloudy and cold, if God has given you the opportunity to see a new day today, the sun will shine upon you and will warm you up.

Do not let any situation load you up with discouragement. If you fall down, get up. If you are sad, find a way to be happy. Come to Jesus. Grab God's hands and let him swing you up in the air as a father does to his child. Bring to God a flower and He will explain to you the meaning of it.

God is real! God is real, my friend! Do not let the devil steal the blessing that God has prepared for you. Be patient, the calm will come. Jesus has the power to stop storms and heavy winds. He is the same now as when He opened the path in the middle of the sea and provided food and water in the desert for His children. He hung on the cross with you in His mind. He saw

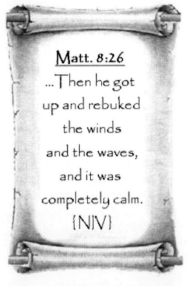

Matt. 8:26

... Then he got up and rebuked the winds and the waves, and it was completely calm.

{NIV}

you before you were born. Jeremiah 1:5 says, "Before I formed you in the womb I knew you, before you were born I set you apart. . . ." {NIV}

He has promised to come back. Jesus said, "Do not let your hearts be troubled. Trust in God; trust also in me. In my Father's house are many rooms; if it were not so, I would have told you. I am going there to prepare a place for you. And if I go and prepare a place for you, **I will come back** and take you to be with me that you also may be where I am. You know the way to the place where I am going." John 14:1-4 {NIV}(Emphasis added) God is real!

In John 14:23 Jesus said, ". . . If anyone loves me, he will obey my teaching. My Father will love him, and we will come to him and make our home with him." {NIV}

Many people have asked me, "How can you be happy and smiling all of the time? Don't all those things that have happened to you in your life affect you?" My answer is this. God is God and now when problems come to me, I send them to Jesus. Jesus knows how to take care of all those problems very well. From the bottom of my heart I want to tell you to trust in the Lord our God and give your life to Jesus, no matter if your heart or family is falling apart. Jesus has the power to fix every broken heart and gather separated families back together. It is okay to fall down, but it's not okay to stay down. Let's get up and fix our eyes on God. He will provide for all your needs according to His riches and glory. Let's kick satan out of our lives and praise God with all our hearts.

The Invitation

If this story has touched something in your heart, I invite you to open the door of your heart to invite Jesus to come in and be the Savior of your life. Simply read the following prayer, mean it from your heart and Jesus will be with you for the rest of your days on earth and forever in eternity.

"Father, in the name of Jesus, I admit that I have sinned, but believe that Jesus died on the cross to save me from my sins and came to give me eternal, abundant life. I ask You to forgive me as I confess Jesus Christ as my Lord and Savior. Save me from my sins and come into my heart and make me a brand new person on the inside, so I can live life the way You intended from this day forward. In Jesus name I pray, Amen."

I praise God for all the lives he has saved through this writing, especially yours. Now, read God's word in the Bible, find a church where you can learn more about the grace of God and praise the Lord all the days of your life.

See the mountains? Many times there are clouds over them, but when the sun shines over them they look beautiful. Let God see you. Let him shine over you. Let God be your sun. Let God be your shelter. Let God be your food and your water. Let God be your good friend. Find in God the smile that you have lost. Find in God the friendship that you don't have. Be rich, be famous. Let God live in your heart.

I have so many more things that I would like to share with you. Maybe this will be on another occasion. For now the desire of my heart is that with these few pages, God has touched your heart in a special way and let you know that He is real, that He loves you no matter how broken your heart is or how many wrong things you have done.

You are beautiful. God loves you and I do, too. Be blessed. Amen.

Acknowledgements

To the Father, the Son, and to the Holy Spirit, Thank You for never forsaking me. Thank You for lifting me up from dust. Thank You for healing my soul and my entire body and for providing water, food, shelter, and protection for me and my family. Thank You for Your presence and Your anointing love that always flows over me. Thank You for being the center of my life, for this project, and the guidance of any plans that will come.

To You be the Glory, Honor, and all the Praise.

To my dear Father and Mother, I do not have enough words to express my deep appreciation and thankfulness for all your sacrifices, efforts, and prayers that touched God's heart to have mercy on me to heal myself and to protect your lives from danger and illness. Dad and Mom, you divided the pain, anguish, tears, and all things in equal measurements to carry over your shoulders. The strongest support besides God in my life came from both of you. Thanks for the honor of being your son and the privilege to call you my parents. You felt the pain of my birth, you saw me grow, you saw me walk, you saw me lose my walk, you saw me walk again. You suffered the tortures of the weather, starvation and the sun's heat, uncovering yourselves so you could cover me. What I most appreciate from you and which has no price is that you sacrificed yourselves to protect me and went through many other things that I will never know. Dad, you are so awesome. Thank you for sharing with me many things that hurt your heart, but for the blessing and encouragement to others are written down in this book. I also extend my thankfulness to all my brothers, sisters and to my Uncle Luis for all their love and support.

My best and deepest thankfulness to **Joan and Don Cardoza** for your moral, spiritual, and physical support. Thank you for your long hours, days, weeks, and months working by my side. And most of all your infinite love. Thanks for all the jars of tears that you have shed with me as I was writing this journal. Thank you for your hospitality and encouragement. Thank you for not letting me be down when I wanted to give up the writing of this journal that reopened the wounds of my soul. God bless you.

Jesse Fuller, thank you for those many hours that you spent with me at the coffee tables of Hillside Market. Thank you for your patience and for your valuable time that you dedicated to listening to me as I shared with you many stories of the journal of my life. Thank you, because as you were listening to me, many wounds were healed in my heart. Thank you, Jesse, for planting the seed of this project and the water that you have irrigated to make this project grow. You and your family will eat of the fruit of your hard work. God bless the labor of your hands.

Keith and Nancy Carns, what a blessing to have people like you in my life. Thanks for letting me be close to you. Thank you for sharing your blessings with me. Thank you for your prayers and your constant calls to let me know your love. As I live, I will keep the freshness of the flowers that you have put in my heart and the blessings of the Lord that you have poured over me. The Lord Bless you.

Ed and Julie Lang, I have been blessed under the blessing that the Lord has poured over you. Thank you for your prayers, thank you for covering me under your roof. May the Lord increase your blessings as you share with others what is given to you.

Bob and Suzanna Williams, here I am because you gave me the opportunity of be part of your home. Thanks for trusting in this soul that the Lord had transformed. Thank you for being with me in all situations and especially on those loneliest days of my life for being far away from my family, you were there with me. Receive my blessings and the rewards of the Lord.

Madison and Sunny Rae Seamans, dear brother and sister, I pray that the Lord increases the blessings of your life. Thank you for being part of this project, for your hard work and your prayers. Thanks for your hospitality and love. It is my prayer that God increases your blessings a hundred percent, and heals and prospers whatever you touch.

Jim and Bonnie Trimble and family, oh boy, what a blessing it is to me to be a part of your family! May the Lord recompense you according to his riches in Glory and let you be prosperous all the days of your life.

My best and sincere thankfulness to **Dr. Cody Gunderson,** as my pastor and friend, for your support, for the growth of my spiritual life, and for the opportunities that you gave me to share the wonderful things that God has done in my life with you and your wonderful congregation, and for those many meals that you, your wife Cheryl, your son, and daughters have shared with me. God bless you Pastor Cody Gunderson and your family.

Wayne and Maria Carpenter, thank you my brother and sister for the wonderful support that you have provided me. There are not enough words to thank you for your love and for taking me to those football games that helped me to get out of my saddest days. God bless you.

I extend my best and sincere thankfulness to all my friends, brothers, and sisters of Yosemite Lakes Community Church and to all those that have supported me from other churches in the Los Angeles, California, area. And to all of those whose names I do not remember, but who are in my heart with love. God Bless You.

Appendix

The following appendix is a compilation of photos from José's life. These include pictures of his family, maps of his route travelled to the United States from El Salvador and other notable occasions mentioned in the autobiography.

José has annotated the original photographs and the notes have been transcribed here.

Enjoy!

Victory!
The Life of José M. Mejía

Back row, left to right:
My sister, Herminia
My sister, Catalina
My brother, Pedro

Front row, left to right:
My sister, Jilma
Me in 1972 before I got polio. Cute, isn't it?

This is me, José, 15 years old, not too happy, but alive. Picture was taken for another ID.

Me again in 1998. This picture was taken for my passport the week of my mother's death.

In the back row, my brother, Pedro is holding the
banana bunch, grown in our little orchard, one year
after he escaped the red zone and barely out of the
hospital. The boy holding the baby is my cousin,
Douglas, and his brother, whose dad was killed at the
ranch by a pair of oxen. The children in the front row
from left to right are my sister, Lorena, 11 years old,
my sister Vitelia, my brother Auturo, Jr., 1 year old,
and my sister Cristabal.

Victory!
The Life of José M. Mejia

My sister, Jilma, 18
years old. The pain
of the war still in
her heart

My brother, Pedro,
a little before he
was recruited by
the guerrilla.

My brother, Arturo, Jr., ready
for his first day of school.

Left to right: Mom, Vitelia, Cristabel,
and dad, my hero.

From left to right: Dad, my sister Lorena, and mom.

Victory!
The Life of José M. Mejia

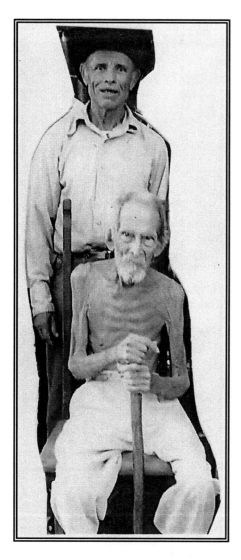

Standing is my Uncle Luis. Seated is my Uncle Luis' father and my dad's step father, Sabastian Chavez. This picture was taken about a month after the invasion when my family's house was burned up. You can see how starvation had consumed their bodies. Just their skin was holding their bones together. I would say that they had already gained some weight back when this picture was taken.

Victory!
The Life of José M. Mejia

This is my dad about a year after he escaped from the red zone. He still has his old stained hat. I never remember seeing my dad mad. He shows what he is to anyone.

My brother, Arturo, Jr. and my nephew, Erick, enjoying life and wearing their best pair of shoes.

Victory!
The Life of José M. Mejia

This is my dad after living four years at the ranch. God had blessed us. In the background is the orchard we had planted and many chickens.

This is my dad at the new place after we moved out from the ranch. He is not a musician, but in his heart he has more music than that keyboard.

Victory!
The Life of José M. Mejia

This is me, three months after I entered the Untied States, trying to learn to play my ten dollar guitar to praise the Lord.

This is my sister, Catalina, and I, six months after I came to the U.S. Alive for the Glory of the Lord and the beauty of the sky.

My brother, Arturo, Jr. with his horse in El
Salvador in 2004.

Here I am, in the U.S. in 2007, riding a
wild horse who dropped me off,
repeating my donkey story.

Here I am praising the Lord with the sound of congas and with a happy and thankful heart.

Praising the Lord with my good friend, Dean Dew, and sister in Christ, Sunny Rae. This is my first time playing bass guitar in the general service at Yosemite Lakes Community Church, Coarsegold, CA.

Victory!
The Life of José M. Mejia

Proud to have earned my high school diploma.

Here I am giving my speech at graduation.

My best teacher and friend, Bobbie Savolskis(second from right) with my graduating class on June 6, 2006

Victory!
The Life of José M. Mejía

Here are all the Trophies that the Lord gave me at the end of my high school journey.

Here I am at Yosemite Lakes Community Church
sharing with the congregation what the Lord has
done in my life.

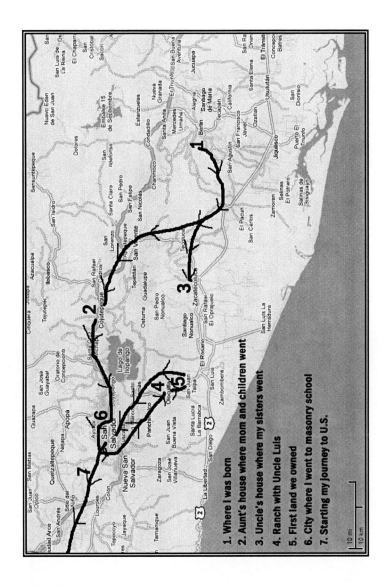

1. Where I was born
2. Aunt's house where mom and children went
3. Uncle's house where my sisters went
4. Ranch with Uncle Luis
5. First land we owned
6. City where I went to masonry school
7. Starting my journey to U.S.

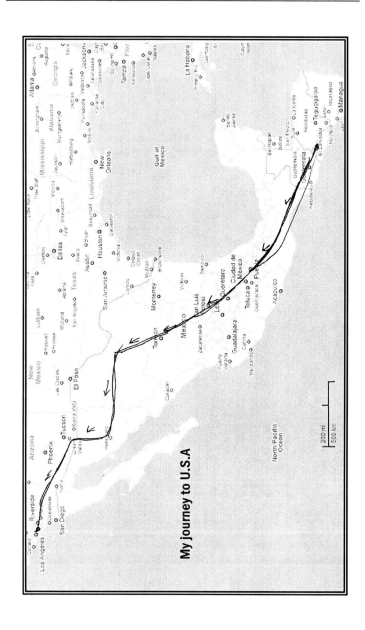

My journey to U.S.A

Post Script

I encourage all of you who read this to take a few minutes to meet the man to whom this story belongs. As a testament to the goodness that replaced the fear and revenge that attempted to take José's heart, the following testimonials reveal a man who has been transformed. They are comments from just a few of many who have met José and whose lives were impacted by the physical demonstration of his faith.

"The hardest thing we've ever been asked to do is to write a few words about who José Mejia is to us. Because he means so much to us, it is difficult to write only a few words. To know José has been a blessing beyond measure. His faith, honesty, integrity, humility are simply a part of his being, not something he works at achieving. Over the years of our friendship, we have shared smiles, laughter, hugs, prayers and enough tears to fill a lake, especially now during the preparation of his book for print. We call him friend, but in our hearts he is so much more than that. He is our son and our brother, mentoring us in many ways. He readily shares all that he has with those around him. He has taught us so much about life, faith, family and the country that saw him born. And from José's example, we pray we will continue our journey daily to be more like Christ.

And like Christ, we know José will also be a part of our lives forever."

Don and Joan Cardoza

      "Some people are impressed with and idolize movie stars, famous athletes or rock stars. Well, I am moved by men of God like José Mejia. José is very special to me and my wife. About five years ago, José's testimony at our church drew us to him. We wanted to know him better and hear about his close walk with the Lord. To know José personally is such a blessing in our lives. In José you find a man so filled with the Holy Spirit and the Word of God that good fruit is all that falls from his "tree." When talking with José, you will be impressed with the fact that nothing negative or gossip comes from his heart, he has only love for his fellow man and the mission God has placed before him. Exalting Jesus and helping our Dear Lord bring in the harvest of souls for our Lord's Kingdom is what drives José. He truly has many gifts and God does not intend to waste them. I love his work ethic, drive and passion. My wife nicknamed him "the new Paul." What a blessing! May God's hand remain on him always. Thank you Lord Jesus for our dear friend and brother, José Mejia."

Sincerely with love and respect,

Wayne and Maria Carpenter

Victory!
The Life of José M. Mejia

"José Mejia has embarked on many journeys, one of which is education. As a lifelong learner he will be prepared to take any road into his future. It was a privilege and joy to work with someone so passionate about his endeavors."

Roberta Savolskis

"Who is José? How about, once in a lifetime friend, adventurous, always cheerful and loved by all. Close friends are hard to come by and José makes friendship fun. He is always willing to try something new. Whether it's camping in the mountains, a trip to the lake, operating a backhoe or hunting Easter eggs for the first time. If the question is, 'José would you like to ....?' the answer is always, 'Yes!' And whether we are working or playing, José is laughing and smiling. That's what makes him so contagious. José is a welcome part of our family. I am impressed with his accomplishments and proud to call him my close friend. We love you José!"

Jim and Bonnie Trimble

Victory!
The Life of José M. Mejia

"José Mejia is an inspiration to all who know him. He walks into a room and his smile, glowing with the love of Jesus Christ, is all over his face. Through hearing all that José endured and sacrificed in his lifetime, he has warmth and genuine love for Jesus Christ. He is a testimony to us all of how complete dependency on God has blessed him through his faithfulness and mercy on his life. The miracles in his life are living proof. Not everyday does God send someone like José into your life and it is my privilege to call him my friend."

Brenda Heckman

"José is one of the Godliest men I know, a man of great faith and integrity. I am honored to call him friend and am grateful God allowed him to touch my life."

Nancy Carns

"José Mejia is a young man in whom the Spirit of God works mightily. My wife and I have had the honor and privilege of knowing José for almost 10 years. I'm sure that José's story will thrill you; however, just being with José is really special. The

Victory!
The Life of José M. Mejia

Lord Jesus Christ has gifted José to serve as an evangelist. Solomon wrote ".... he who wins souls is wise." Prov. 11:30b {NIV}. José has great wisdom. José both spoke and served as Spanish/English translator with a ministry team from Yosemite Lakes Community Church for chapel services at the Madera Rescue Mission in Madera, California. At Mission chapel services over a five year period, more than 2,000 souls asked our Heavenly Father to forgive their sins and receive eternal life through the blood of our God and Savior, Jesus Christ. I'm looking forward to spending lots of time with José in Heaven."

Keith Carns

There is no clinical diagnosis that can explain what has brought José to where he is now. The only explanation is a divine revelation and personal relationship with a power that most of us will never fully understand. Perhaps José's story will help us all comprehend the true meaning of faith, gratitude and an appreciation for the very essence of life. Whether you believe in a superior being, a god or the Living God, this story will stir the very core of your soul and you will wrestle with the conflict that is your maker's calling and the world's condition.

José, I thank you for the honor and privilege of serving God through your struggle and victory. I am forever indebted to you for your love and friendship.

Jesse Fuller

About the Author

José M. Mejia is a plumber by trade, an evangelist by choice and now, a first time author. Since the completion of his journal that later became this book, José once again followed the calling of the Lord. He took his ministry back to southern California, where he shared the Gospel with his family and friends and everyone who listened.

His journey will not end there. José has heard the Lord calling him once again. This time José will be returning to the country that saw him born, El Salvador. Although, his mission from God has not yet been totally revealed to him, it's enough for José to know that returning to his country is a part of God's plan for his life.

Many lives have been saved and will be saved in the future because of José's decision, so many years ago, to obey God's calling in **all** circumstances.

By the Grace of God, the smile he wears today will never again be wiped from his face.

Joan Cardoza

To contact the Author, email:

victoryreply@yahoo.com

Personal Notes

Personal Notes

Breinigsville, PA USA
06 August 2010
243085BV00001B/2/P